POSTGRADUATE STUDY IN DEVELOPING AREAS:

A ROUGH GUIDE

Second Edition

Edited by

Elsbeth Robson and Katie Willis

Monograph No.9
Developing Areas Research Group
Royal Geographical Society
(with The Institute of British Geographers)

1997

Published 1997 by the Developing Areas Research Group (DARG)
of the Royal Geographical Society
(with The Institute of British Geographers)

ISBN 0 946689 10 5

Produced by Keele University Press. Tel. 01782 584215

Dedication

To the memory of Amy Biehl
26 year old U.S. postgraduate student murdered
in Guguletu Township, Cape Town, South Africa
25th August 1993
'...because she forgot she was white'
(Sunday Times 27.4.94)

Contents

Page

List of Contributors vi

Introduction 1

PART I

1.   The Logistics of Undertaking Field Research in 'Developing Areas'
     Sally Lloyd Evans with Elsbeth Robson and Katie Willis ...7

2.   Methodological Issues in Overseas Fieldwork: Experiences from
     Nicaragua's Northern Atlantic Coast
     Sarah Howard 19

3.   Flexibility, Funding and Foresight: Tips for the Physical Geographer
     in Developing Areas Research
     Georgina Endfield and Peter W. O'Connor...................38

4.   From Teacher to Taxi Driver: Reflections on Research Roles in
     Developing Areas
     Elsbeth Robson 51

5.   Home, Abroad, Home: The Challenges of Postgraduate Fieldwork
     'At Home'
     Uwem Ite..75

6.   Alternative Affiliations and the Personal Politics of Overseas
     Research: Some Reflections
     Simon Batterbury 85

7.   Ethics of Research in the Third World
     Clare Madge 113

8.   Letter from the Field: Reflections Half-Way Through
     Nuala Bryce Gormley 125

PART II *PRACTICAL TIPS*

Elsbeth Robson and **Katie Willis** with **Becky Elmhirst**

9.   Looking after Yourself: Health Issues 135

10. Taking Care and Just in Case: Safety and Insurance 139

11. From Money to Mosquito Nets: Ideas for Packing
     Your Rucksack 148

12. Keeping Sane: Life in the Field 154

13. Useful References: Reading, Addresses and Funding 162

List of Contributors

Simon Batterbury is a lecturer in geography at Brunel University and formerly a doctoral student at the Graduate School of Geography, Clark University. His fieldwork, on the cultural ecology of the Mossi, was conducted in co-operation with environmental projects in northern Burkina Faso. He is now researching social and environmental change in Southwest Niger, and urban transport issues in West London.

    Simon Batterbury, Department of Geography and Earth Science, Brunel University, Uxbridge, Middlesex, UB8 3PH.

    Email: simon.batterbury@brunel.ac.uk

Becky Elmhirst began research in Indonesia in 1986 for a BA dissertation at the University of Newcastle-upon-Tyne on gender divisions in the informal labour market in Jakarta. After a masters degree at the University of British Columbia, Canada and three years as a journalist in the UK, she returned to Indonesia in 1994, this time to Sumatra, for doctoral research on a political ecology of the transmigration programme. She is a lecturer in geography at the University of Brighton. She hopes to continue research on gender, environment and development in Southeast Asia.

    Department of Construction, Geography and Surveying, University of Brighton, Mithras House, Lewes Road, Brighton, BN2 4AT.

    Email: R.J.Elmhirst@bton.ac.uk

Georgina Endfield is a postgraduate student at the Sheffield Centre for International Drylands Research, University of Sheffield. As part of her Ph.D. she carried out research in central Mexico between September 1995 and May 1996. During nine months overseas she investigated environmental change since the Spanish Conquest, through archival and documentary media and field evidence. She hopes to continue this research in the future.

    Department of Geography, University of Sheffield, Sheffield, S10 2TN.

    Email: G.H.Endfield@Sheffield.ac.uk

Nuala Bryce Gormley is a postgraduate student in the Geography Department at the University of Edinburgh. When her contribution was written, she was carrying out field research for her thesis on 'mission and development', while working as a volunteer teacher in Maracha, in the West Nile region of Uganda.
Department of Geography, University of Edinburgh,
Drummond Street, Edinburgh, EH8 9PX.
Email: nbg@ed.ac.uk

Sarah Howard spent thirteen months in Nicaragua between 1990 and 1991 carrying out doctoral research on regional autonomy, ethnicity, land and development among the Miskitu Indian people of the North Atlantic Autonomous Region. Since then she has completed two short pieces of research in Nicaragua examining issues of indigenous and peasant livelihoods, conservation issues and land conflicts in the Bosawás rainforest reserve. During the second visit she became the intermediary with the Nicaraguan authorities when an NGO worker with whom she was travelling was 'detained' by former *Contra* resistance fighters. In April and May 1996 she conducted research with Tim Acott in the Annapurna Himal into the impacts of ecotourism on local communities. She is a lecturer in geography at the University of Greenwich.
School of Earth and Environmental Science, University of
Greenwich, Medway Campus, Pembroke, Chatham Maritime,
Kent ME4 4AW.

Uwem Ite is a lecturer in geography at Lancaster University and has field experience in Nigeria, where he researched (1992-1995) for his PhD on agriculture and tropical forest conservation. His research interests in environment and development in sub-Saharan Africa focus on natural resources management, environmental impact assessment and social sustainability. He has recently advised multinational mining corporations operating in Nigeria, Colombia, South Africa and the Philippines on the problems and challenges of community relations and development.
Department of Geography, Lancaster University, Lancaster,
LA1 4YB.
Email: u.ite@lancaster.ac.uk

Sally Lloyd Evans, having lived in Mexico City in the early 1980s, worked at the University of the West Indies for twelve months between 1990 and 1992 whilst undertaking fieldwork for a Ph.D. on ethnicity and gender in the informal sector. She is a lecturer in the Department of Geography at Reading University where she continues to undertake research in the Caribbean.
Department of Geography, Reading University, Whiteknights, P.O. Box 227, Reading, RG6 2AB.
Email: S.Lloyd-evans@reading.ac.uk

Clare Madge is a lecturer in human geography at the University of Leicester. She undertook Ph.D. research in The Gambia, where she investigated the multiple roles that minor forest products played in rural households. Since then, she has been involved in two research projects: on women's indigenous domestic knowledge in The Gambia and research in conjunction with Leicester City Council on gender, space and public parks in Leicester.
Department of Geography, Leicester University, Leicester, LE1 7RH.
Email: cm12@leicester.ac.uk.

Peter O'Connor is a postgraduate student at the Sheffield Centre for International Drylands Research, University of Sheffield. In 1995, he spent two months in Zambia and Namibia undertaking research for his Ph.D on climatic change and establishing the former extent of the Kalahari Desert. He has also travelled to other countries in southern Africa and has other research interests in Crete. In the future he hopes to continue his research on Quaternary environmental change in developing countries.
Department of Geography, University of Sheffield, Sheffield, S10 2TN.
Email: P.W.Oconnor@Sheffield.ac.uk

Contributors

Elsbeth Robson, having done voluntary work in East Africa, first did research overseas in 1988 for her B.Sc. dissertation on peri-urban development in Kenya. Between 1991 and 1993 she spent fifteen months in Northern Nigeria researching for a D.Phil. on gender and peasant households. She has travelled to other countries of West Africa and is continuing her interests in developing countries by planning student fieldtrips to Kenya and embarking on research in Zimbabwe. She is a lecturer in Development Studies at Keele University.

Department of Geography, Keele University, Keele, Staffs, ST5 5BG.
Email: gea06@keele.ac.uk

Katie Willis spent twelve months in Oaxaca City Mexico between 1990 and 1993, carrying out fieldwork for an M.Phil. and D.Phil. on women's employment and social networks. Since then she has carried out further research in Mexico and Singapore. She is a lecturer in the Department of Geography at the University of Liverpool.

Department of Geography, University of Liverpool, Roxby Building, P.O. Box 147, Liverpool, L69 3BX.
Email: kwillis@liverpool.ac.uk

INTRODUCTION

Each year a proportion of geography postgraduates at UK higher education institutions undertake extended periods of field research in 'developing' countries. Frequently they are inadequately prepared for the realities and practicalities of such fieldwork, which presents particular problems for several reasons. First, the necessarily long duration of fieldwork and immersion in the often 'foreign' field environment; secondly, the poor (if not impossible) communication with supervisors during the fieldwork period, and thirdly, the general difficulties of working in 'developing' countries. There still appears to be, particularly among supervisors, an all too common 'sink or swim' attitude towards such fieldwork, which advocates that postgraduates should learn by their mistakes. As postgraduates rarely receive any specific training for undertaking research in the so-called 'Third World', despite ESRC (Economic and Social Research Council) demands for postgraduate training, students are forced to cope 'in situ' with practical and ethical problems which (nearly always) arise. When students set off for Mongolia or Botswana, supervisors often appear to be more concerned about whether they have a good grasp of theory and a well-written literature review, than ensuring they are well prepared for the rigours of fieldwork. Students are expected to go through a kind of 'baptism by fire' in the field - probably mirroring supervisors' own experiences. Such attitudes are unnecessary and unhelpful. We hope this monograph will help students be more aware of the pitfalls of doing fieldwork in 'developing' areas and thus be in a stronger position to tackle them.

As postgraduate students who undertook research in 'Third World' countries as outsiders, we became very aware of the difficulties that arise throughout the fieldwork process - in the planning stages, during work in the field and on return 'home' to Britain. Discussions with other graduates showed that we were not alone in the problems we experienced with fieldwork and our unpreparedness for the realities of carrying out research in 'developing' areas. With these matters in mind, and following the suggestion of the previous Postgraduate Representative on the DARG Committee, Sally Lloyd Evans, a DARG/Postgraduate Forum session at the 1994 IBG Annual Conference in Nottingham was held as a forum for discussing issues of fieldwork, with presentations by Reg Cline-Cole, Sally Lloyd Evans, Sarah Howard, Clare Madge, Elsbeth Robson and James Sidaway. This proved to be a very successful event but it was felt that, as the session reached only the limited conference-attending audience, the contributions could have greater usefulness if accessible to more postgraduates and their supervisors. The purpose of the first edition of this monograph was, therefore, to make the presentations more widely available, together with other information better distributed in written form.

Following the success of the first edition, which sold in several countries, we decided, in conjunction with the DARG Committee, to produce a second edition. This has enabled us to update the original material and to address the two main omissions in the first edition: physical geography fieldwork and reflections on doing research 'at home'. We have also included a section on road traffic accidents in the safety section by Becky Elmhirst who has contributed her reflections on the issue based on her own experiences.

We realise that postgraduates going to the field can never be totally prepared for every eventuality, but much useful preparation can be done. It is our hope that this monograph will continue to provide useful information and pointers to help avoid common problems, so that students can attempt to maximise the academic usefulness and rewards of fieldwork. To achieve this aim, the papers in this monograph make both general points about doing fieldwork and discuss specific cases and examples to illustrate the diversity, as well as the commonalities, of fieldwork experiences.

Although directed particularly at those undertaking research in 'developing' areas at postgraduate level, the contents here may also be useful to other 'first timers', for example, undergraduates doing dissertations. We do not pretend that we have all the answers, but hope to give at least some hints to those contemplating the challenge of fieldwork in 'developing' areas.

This monograph is structured in two parts. Part I consists of the papers presented in Nottingham, with the exception of the joint paper by Reg Cline-Cole and James Sidaway which was considered to be more suitable for publication elsewhere. Chapters by Simon Batterbury, Nuala Bryce Gormley, Uwem Ite and Georgina Endfield and Peter O'Connor are also included. Simon's chapter was written in response to discussion following the IBG conference presentations, while Nuala's chapter is in the form of a letter to prospective fieldworkers as she was in Uganda doing fieldwork and could not be present at the conference. Uwem's chapter on research 'at home' and Georgina and Peter's chapter on physical geography fieldwork were written especially for the second edition.

The first chapter by Sally Lloyd Evans with Elsbeth Robson and Katie Willis, deals with the many logistical and practical aspects involved in successfully completing useful and enjoyable fieldwork. Many handy tips are outlined for prospective researchers going afield. In the second chapter, Sarah Howard draws on her own experiences in Nicaragua to discuss some of the methodological aspects of undertaking empirical research - often very problematic in so-called 'Third World' countries and frequently not proceeding as smoothly as one might expect from the textbooks. Georgina Endfield and Peter O'Connor highlight the particular issues involved in physical geography fieldwork in the fourth chapter. The roles which outside researchers find themselves in are discussed by Elsbeth Robson, who reflects on her personal experiences of fieldwork in West Africa, where she was everything from teacher to taxi driver. The following chapter by Uwem Ite is a consideration of fieldwork from a different viewpoint; that of a researcher 'going home' to Nigeria to study. Simon Batterbury then considers the institutional umbrellas for students to carry out research in 'developing' areas away from their home institutions. In particular, he examines the opportunities offered by the development agency sector for students to do practicable and relevant research and encourages creativity in affiliation. The chapter by Clare Madge examines some of the complicated ethics of doing research in developing contexts and ponders on her own research experiences in The Gambia. Finally, Nuala Bryce Gormley's letter from the field gives a few hot tips and pragmatic insights into living the realities of fieldwork.

Part II of the monograph is composed of several sections dealing with different practical matters of fieldwork execution. Common-sense advice is given on health matters, safety and insurance, and equipment. In *Life in the Field* some suggestions are made about coping with a long stay in an unfamiliar culture. The final section consists of an extended list of suggested further reading covering methodology and 'how to do it' guides, as well as descriptions of fieldwork experiences and useful addresses for specialist advice and funding sources.

We would like to thank the DARG committee for their continued encouragement and support in the preparation of this second edition. We are especially grateful to the contributors to the 1994 IBG conference session whose papers appear here, to the authors of the other papers for their willingness to contribute, and to everyone whose comments on the first edition were so helpful in the compilation of the second.

Our thanks are due to people whose reading lists were useful in compiling the references section - especially Marcus Banks, Louise Crewe, Michelle Lowe and David Simon. Also Simon Batterbury provided information on U.S. funding sources. The help of Margaret Willis with word processing is also gratefully acknowledged. Warm thanks go also to Lisa Matchett and Martin Rimmer whose artistic talents produced the cartoons.

We do not claim that all the information here is completely accurate. Any corrections, additions, comments or suggestions which might be incorporated in a future edition would be very welcome and should be made to the authors or the DARG Publications Editor c/o RGS-IBG, Kensington Gore, London, SW7 2AR.

We, the editors, remain firmly of the opinion that, despite all the practical and ethical problems of research in 'developing' areas by foreign postgraduates, it is a worthwhile enterprise if carried out sensitively and thoughtfully. Not least, cross-cultural research can counter tendencies towards ethnocentric or universalist views and can help to deconstruct distinctions between 'here' and 'there', or 'us' and 'them'.

Elsbeth Robson and Katie Willis
Keele & Liverpool
March 1997

'At last the ultimate guide to fieldwork!'

PART I

1.

THE LOGISTICS OF UNDERTAKING FIELDWORK IN 'DEVELOPING AREAS'

Sally Lloyd Evans with Elsbeth Robson & Katie Willis[1]

INTRODUCTION

A Ph.D. is not just an academic piece of work, it is a learning process which encourages the development of many practical skills. The organisation of Ph.D. research is particularly important when fieldwork involves an extended stay in a 'developing country'. In addition to the usual strains of postgraduate life, researchers may suddenly find themselves alone in a new environment. Once in the field, there is often little supervisory or departmental back-up, or assistance from family and friends. The success of the project often revolves around the ability of the researcher to work alone within a new setting. Even the simple tasks of finding somewhere safe and suitable to live, or arranging transport, require a great deal of work and effort. It is, therefore, a life-shaping process, which will probably provide some of the most memorable life experiences, as well as those which are better left forgotten.

Field preparation for working in a 'developing country' differs between individuals, often according to the level of pre-established contacts held by a supervisor, department or the student him/herself. Some research students are fortunate to be offered a great deal of support before embarking on their journey, others are not. It is the intention of this chapter to offer some useful insights into the practicalities of undertaking fieldwork in a 'developing area', by drawing upon our own experiences. The destinations of research students obviously vary a great deal, so some of the factors discussed here will not be relevant to everyone.

This chapter is divided into two sections and explores a number of familiar obstacles associated with undertaking research in 'developing countries'. Firstly, we deal with the preparatory stage of the research, including the search to establish contacts, find accommodation and acquire

---

[1] This is based on the paper given by Sally Lloyd Evans at the 1994 IBG Annual Conference, but has been expanded by the author and the editors.

visas or permits. Then we move on to discuss the practicalities once 'in the field' drawing from our own experiences in Trinidad, Mexico and Nigeria.

FIELDWORK PREPARATION

When working in a 'developing country', the best laid plans may go wrong, so researchers need to be flexible. Planning field research needs to start early as communications may be difficult and, for local institutions, responding to a request for information from an overseas student is unlikely to be at the top of their priorities. Therefore, establishing a number of varied local contacts is often a good way to start fieldwork preparation.

Establishing Contacts

Colleagues and supervisors may have good links with a university or other institution in the research area but if not, the researcher needs to make his/her own contacts. A good plan is to obtain affiliation to a university or research centre which might be interested in the project. Although this may take several months of correspondence, a letter from a local institution will often assist in obtaining a visa or student entry permit. More importantly, it often acts as a key document in a range of circumstances, which range from gaining access to government ministries, to getting out of trouble! Some kind of official affiliation may prove to be more useful than a visa. Sally was once detained at an airport, and it was her letter of affiliation which convinced the officials to allow her entry to the country. It can also be used a proof of the validity of the research, and may help in securing accommodation, or even hiring a car. Simon Batterbury discusses the issues surrounding institutional affiliation in more detail later in this volume.

In addition to obtaining official assistance, it is useful to make a note of colleagues' friends, relations and other contacts who live in the area. One might be initially reluctant to visit a friend's elderly relative, for example, but in our experience personal contacts of this nature can prove to be a valuable support network in the field. Such contacts may also be helpful in other ways e.g. interviews with senior officials may be more willingly granted if the name of a shared acquaintance is offered. In return, be prepared, when asked, to take gifts (which in the Caribbean usually seems to be tea, Marmite or pepper sauce) to various relatives and acquaintances.

On a more serious note, it is often essential to enlist assistance of other institutions associated with the research, such as the various agencies of the United Nations or non-governmental organisations (NGOs). This process involves writing numerous letters. Be prepared for few official responses, although this does not necessarily mean that they will not remember you if later you present yourself at their office.

Official Documentation : Visa & Permit Acquisition

Another immediate task of fieldwork preparation is to enquire about the need for visas or work permits. Obviously, this differs according to location and length of stay. In many cases, a local affiliation may be required in order to obtain a visa. Enquiries need to be made early, as it may take several months to go through the necessary bureaucratic procedures. Addresses for Embassies and High Commissions can be obtained by telephone from Directory Enquiries, or from travel guidebooks. The whole visa procedure can be remarkably time-consuming and may require a great deal of patience. If you do not want to and/or are unable to spend time travelling and queuing to deal with embassy bureaucracy, it is possible to use a visa agency. For a small fee, they will deal with all the hassles and complete the paperwork. In Britain, visa agencies include The Visaservice and Thomas Cook.[2]

'Upon request for his paperwork, Bob produced a 'flying swan', this although realistic was not good enough for customs.'

---

[2] For addresses see Chapter 13 *Useful References.*

There are also ethical issues involved when applying for visas. Should you apply for a research visa when you know it is going to be difficult and could in all likelihood get away with a tourist visa? If/when a research visa/permission is refused should you continue with the research project? These are difficult questions (see the Porteous and Dobson debate in Area 1988).

It is useful to check whether the Foreign and Commonwealth Office has any restrictions on the area, or offers any particular advice to travellers. If the country of destination is on one of their 'red lists' for areas deemed unsafe, then funding agencies and universities often require students to postpone their fieldtrip until the area is regarded as safe for foreign travellers.

Make sure that your passport is still valid and that it will cover your entire stay plus a few months. If you are travelling through a number of countries, make sure that your passport has enough empty pages for visas etc. As many countries require vaccination certificates before you are allowed to enter, it is a good idea to keep these certificates inside your passport with an elastic band to prevent everything falling out.

Health and Medical Requirements
Check up on vaccine requirements well in advance of your trip. Further advice about the health aspects of fieldwork are covered in Chapter 9 *Health Issues.*

Funding Overseas Fieldwork
Many postgraduates have to seek funding for the fieldwork involved in their postgraduate work. Several points should be remembered:
1. There is money but it does not grow on trees - you have to make an effort (sometimes a lot of effort) to get it. Fund-raising is very competitive.
2. To maximise your chances of getting your share you must start early and be very organised to keep copies of everything, scrupulously observe application deadlines and apply for everything there is going.
3. If in doubt about your eligibility for funds from a particular source do not just forget it - phone and ask and if in doubt make an application anyway because it just might be successful.
4. Fund-raising is time consuming, but it should not become a distraction from the research itself.
5. Persevere and don't give up!

If you receive financial support for your degree, then the grant agency (ESRC, NERC etc.) is the obvious place to start the search for fieldwork funding. However, they require students to submit fully-priced and itemised fieldwork budgets months in advance, funds may not be disbursed until receipts are submitted and may take considerable time to be processed. There are certain items which will usually not be funded, such as the purchase of expensive equipment, hiring research assistants and photocopying. However, there is always room for negotiation. For example, if you are undertaking a questionnaire survey and photocopying costs are high in the field, then you may be able to get a refund on the production of receipts. Check the award handbook and fieldwork expense claim forms for details and if in doubt, phone and ask. For some items, it may be impossible to obtain receipts. If this is the case, ask a colleague in the field, or your supervisor to write a letter explaining the situation and confirming that the claim you have submitted is a fair reflection of the costs incurred.

Universities may have funds offered especially for graduate students, equipment, travel, expeditions or conference attendance. Check with your university offices and the head of department. In collegiate universities, funds may be available from colleges. Student unions, especially their welfare sections, may be able to tell you what funds are available from within, or outside the university. Read notice boards in your students' union, department or college where details of funds may be posted. Try your local reference library too. Careers offices have handbooks and directories of grant bodies. There are a number of grants available to geographers. These and some other award details are listed in Chapter 13 *Useful References*.

Getting There - Cheap Fares
Campus Travel and STA are two travel agents with offices around the country who specialise in cheap airline tickets especially for students. Also try your student union travel shop. Trailfinders is another company geared towards the needs of the 'independent traveller'. Some travel agents specialise in tickets to certain regions - Journey Latin America and Austravel, for example. It is also possible to obtain reduced fares through travel agents offering cut-price services to those involved in 'development' work. One such company is Key Travel (see Chapter 13 *Useful Addresses* for details). Look at newspaper adverts for cheap fares advertised by bucket shops which are not all disreputable - most are ABTA and ATOL members. Postgraduates have been known to get full-fare quotations from the airline which is then paid for by the student's funding body, so allowing for two trips to the field on bucket shop tickets. This may enable you to carry out an initial familiarisation trip prior to the main period of field research. Some funding agencies now offer two trips because of the advantages such an arrangement gives to the student, so make enquiries.

However, be careful with cheap tickets as they may be less flexible in terms of refunds or schedule changes; they may arrive or depart at anti-social times, or only on awkward days of the week. A very cheap flight may be with a little-known airline that only has a couple of planes and reaches the destination via an obscure route, taking longer than the direct route. If your funding body is paying your fare then you might as well go safely and comfortably.

Accommodation
Of prime concern in considering accommodation during fieldwork is where YOU are going to feel most comfortable, safe and able to work effectively. If you are carrying out a project which involves working with a particular community, you may feel that it would be best for you to live within that community. There are obvious advantages of living in close proximity to the people with whom you are working; you can learn a great deal from just observing and getting involved with everyday activities, and 'fitting in' can be much easier if you live in the area. However, for a number of reasons you may feel that you do not want to live in the district or village where you are working; at least not all the time. Having some space of your own where you feel secure and are left alone, can be very important during fieldwork. You may well need somewhere to retreat to when you want to write or think and where you can 'be yourself', rather than conforming to local behavioural norms.

Trying to make decisions about accommodation is very difficult from a distance, but it can also be daunting to arrive in a new environment without having anywhere to stay. A sensible arrangement is to arrange university or hotel accommodation for the first few weeks and then decide on your long-term plans when the area is more familiar, you have obtained local advice, visited places in person and negotiated over prices. You may have to give your address to immigration officials before you arrive, otherwise you may not be allowed to enter the country. Therefore, even if you do not stay there for the entire period, it is a good idea to have some idea of where you are staying initially.

In searching for accommodation, the local university is often a good starting point, as they will probably be able to offer the best advice as to what is locally available. It may be difficult to obtain a room on campus, but the university may have accommodation for rent elsewhere. Even if living on campus, or near the university is not suitable as a research base, university staff may have good contacts with rural research centres, or be able to assist in finding accommodation in other regions.

Prices of local accommodation in many 'developing areas' may well be much cheaper than in the UK, but not that cheap if it is necessary to stay in accessible city accommodation. In major cities, reasonable accommodation can cost as much as its UK equivalent. Easy accessibility to transport and services is often essential when living alone. In many places, house sharing is not an option for strangers and renting an entire house may prove expensive. Be wary of signing long-term leases for accommodation with UK-based agents, unless you have firm local advice, because on arrival the accommodation may be in an undesirable location or not up to expectations, and breaking legal agreements can be difficult. Hotels are usually too expensive in the long-term and hostels are often too basic for working. For example, writing up research in the evenings requires good light (preferably electric) and power. A phone is often a desirable luxury and may be impossible to obtain, but having access to a phone or even a fax, is very useful for calling supervisors when fieldwork meets obstacles.

Language Learning
If you need language training for your research, then you will have to make preparations well in advance. If you are a beginner, then you should start learning as soon as possible. For widely-spoken languages, you may be able to attend lessons at your college or university, however, for other languages it may be necessary to go elsewhere for tuition. You could also 'teach-yourself' using material from university language labs, or cassettes and books available from public libraries, bookshops or through mail order. Whichever method you choose it will involve an expenditure of both time and money and any expenditure should be included in the fieldwork budget proposals.

Whatever your level of language proficiency, you might feel that an intensive language course on your arrival in the field would be beneficial. For those familiar with the language it could be a refresher course, whereas for beginners, it may be a good way of tuning into local accents and vocabulary. Try and find out about courses before you go, but if this is not possible guidebooks, tourist offices and local colleges are good places to start.

Language is something which many students worry about before they undertake fieldwork. Complete fluency is rarely needed, but you will have to be able to carry out interviews without resorting to a dictionary every few minutes. The longer you stay in the field the better your language skills will get. You should also remember that you can use research assistants and translators if necessary.[3]

---

[3] The issues surrounding the use of translators are discussed by both Sarah Howard and Elsbeth Robson later in this monograph.

'Bob knew his attempts at local pidgin had failed when he was solemnly presented with a hairdryer which didn't look anything like his chicken and green peppers'

ONCE 'IN THE FIELD'
Arriving
International airports are notorious sites for giving travellers problems, particularly when vulnerable and flustered arriving in a new place after a long journey. This is especially the case when having to interact in a different language. If at all possible, when arriving somewhere for the first time, arrange for someone to meet you at the airport.

If this is not possible, it is a good idea to decide before arriving where you are going to stay and have some small change in local currency available, or some smallish denomination travellers cheques/currency to change at the airport. Make sure that you know the exchange rate and reasonable prices for taxis to avoid the possibility of getting 'ripped off'. In many countries, taxi drivers and others at transport termini act as touts for (often seedy) hotels. Beware! Some airports have officially-recognised taxi services - use these. If you have to try your luck it is advisable to know where you want to go, rather than leaving it up to the driver.

If arriving late at night and without anyone to meet you, it might be an idea to try and share a taxi with fellow passengers. Katie did this when she first arrived in Mexico City by approaching a couple of Dutch backpackers who were on the same plane. It worked out well as they could not speak Spanish so were glad for a translator and Katie was able to split the cost of a taxi and have company for the trip to a city centre hotel.

Flexibility and the Research Project
Flexibility is an important quality when working in many 'developing areas'. Researchers should attempt to adjust to the lifestyles of the people they work with and conduct their research accordingly. The nine-to-five working day is often abandoned, particularly when undertaking social research. Instead, interviews may have to be undertaken at 5 a.m. if this suits the participants. Pilot surveys are essential in order to identify appropriate survey times and locations and they are invaluable in establishing an effective survey technique. Although it may be beneficial to enlist whatever assistance is available, the researcher should be prepared to work alone, particularly at the start.

Despite the best-laid plans, many devised at home in the UK, one of the greatest problems is starting the primary data collection. After the initial settling down period, which may have been combined with a library study, there comes a time when the researcher needs to launch into the questionnaire survey or other data gathering. Before attempting to conduct interviews or questionnaires it is a good idea to become familiar with the survey areas, or the communities where you will be working. During Sally's field research, interviewing street traders frequently meant returning from a day's work with two bags of mangoes, having bought one from each trader! Asking questions and learning about a new culture is a good way to make friends and contacts. Networking is often crucial to successful research when investigating unfamiliar and sensitive issues.

Travel

How will you travel around during fieldwork? Will you need to buy, or hire a car for your fieldwork? You may need an international driving licence (check in guide books) which you can get in the UK by taking your driver's licence to an RAC or AA office. It costs £4.00 and is valid for a year, but in some countries you will need to take a local driving test, so find out once you arrive. Public transport is usually the cheapest option for internal travel, but it helps if you have lots of stamina and not too much luggage. It is nearly always a good way to see the country. For convenience, however, you may prefer to have your own vehicle. Funding bodies may not be willing to meet the cost of a car or motorbike, even though it would be cheaper than hiring one, so you should make enquiries before you leave. You should also bear in mind the cost of petrol and any taxes or insurance for which road users are liable.[4]

If you intend to cross an international boundary during your travels, ensure that you have all the appropriate documentation, both for entry into the neighbouring country and for re-entry into the country where you are doing your research. You should be especially careful about the requirements regarding air tickets. We know of someone who was stuck in Guatemala because Mexican officials would not let her re-enter the country without the plane ticket that was left safely in Mexico City. A similar scenario could have happened to Elsbeth returning to Nigeria after attending a conference in Senegal, but she was luckier because she knew the immigration officer who was her friend's uncle.

Obtaining Local Advice and Assistance

Although questions of research ethics are discussed by Clare Madge in her chapter, attention needs to be drawn to a potential obstacle concerning the planning of fieldwork with local researchers or academics. Local assistance is invaluable and advice should be taken concerning personal safety or areas to be avoided. However, beliefs and perceptions of university staff are likely to be based on their own socialisation and culture. Thus, in the Caribbean, for example, some local researchers are often reluctant to enter low-income communities due to their own (often ill-conceived) perceptions of these areas as dangerous or criminal. Images of places are not always correct, and while it would perhaps be unwise for researchers to ignore advice from people who know the area, personal judgement of situations is necessary. In Trinidad, people want to protect 'outsiders' and look after them in their own social groups. A good researcher is often one who can work in all environments with a host of

---

[4] You should also consider safety issues. See Chapter 10.

very different people, providing care is taken to respect the views maintained by different social groups.

Observing Local Codes of Behaviour

Codes of socially-expected behaviour differ from place to place and care should be taken to respect local cultures as far as possible. Dress codes are a very obvious example of things you should be aware of and should seek to adapt to. In some societies, shorts are strictly for the beach and jeans for after work. In the Caribbean, for example, smart dress is often the norm in universities and in government offices. Meeting a local official in casual dress is rarely the best way to obtain assistance, as in many societies this shows a lack of respect. To avoid being hassled in town, particularly for women, it is often a good move to dress smartly and carry a briefcase in order to 'fit in' with other workers.

Certain forms of language, such as slang and swearing, may also be frowned upon. If the local language has different grammatical forms for polite and informal use, make sure that you know the difference and use them appropriately. If in doubt, use the polite form, as people can always tell you that they would prefer informality. In Mexico, Katie always used the polite *Usted* form of the verb, except when talking to children or close friends. As she got to know some of the local residents more closely, she was asked to call them *tú*, which is used in informal settings.

Work

Once you have settled in, it is sensible to formulate a research timetable. It does not have to be very precise, but should provide you with a clear outline of what you will be doing when. Make sure that you give yourself plenty of time to carry out questionnaire surveys or interviews as these rely on others, and make sure that you leave some contingency time at the end (perhaps a couple of weeks), as nobody ever keeps to their timetable. Beware of being over ambitious. For example, questionnaires are very tiring to do, and, although it is physically possible to do interviews from morning 'til night, it is mentally taxing and it may be better interviewing for only part of the day and doing something else for the rest of the time.

Don't forget to timetable free time into your programme. A day off each week will keep you fresh and enable you to socialise and to get to know the local area. You should also try to have some kind of holiday during an extended fieldwork period. Not only will this give you something to look forward to, but travelling broadens your knowledge of the country or region in which you are working, and a break from the fieldwork environment can crystallise ideas.

It is very unlikely that you will be able to have regular contact with your supervisor while in the field. Before you leave for the field, therefore, you should arrange with her/him if, how and when to send work back. Perhaps a monthly update on what you have been doing would provide suitable motivation for you and should keep you supervisor happy. If possible, your supervisor should return the work with comments, so that you can act on them while still in the field. Some funding agencies, such as the ESRC, will fund a short visit for the supervisor if the fieldwork period is a prolonged one. Although the thought of your supervisor coming out to the field to 'check up on you' may strike terror into your heart, it can be very valuable and it also aids student-supervisor relations as the supervisor gets a trip abroad at someone else's expense! It is a good idea to keep re-evaluating your work, so that you can adapt your research while you still have time. Keeping field notebooks and coding questionnaire data as you go along makes everything far more manageable when you leave the field.

CONCLUSIONS

Hopefully this chapter has shed light on some of the practicalities which may need to be faced when working alone in a 'developing country'. As a final note, do not forget to keep in touch with those who provided help and assistance, and keep any promises regarding the sharing of research findings or reports. In conclusion, remember that fieldwork is usually enjoyable, and will probably become one of your most important life experiences.

REFERENCES
Dobson, Belinda 1987 'One of the reasons geography doesn't: A reply to the observations of Porteous and Knight' <u>Area</u> 19, 3, 287.

Porteous, Douglas J. 1986 'Intimate sensing' <u>Area</u> 18, 3, 250-1.

Porteous, Douglas J. 1988 'No excuses, Belinda' <u>Area</u> 20, 1, 72.

2.

METHODOLOGICAL ISSUES IN OVERSEAS FIELDWORK : EXPERIENCES FROM NICARAGUA'S NORTHERN ATLANTIC COAST[1]

Sarah Howard

INTRODUCTION

In this chapter I discuss some of the methodological issues which arose in the course of conducting research in Nicaragua. I begin with a brief description of the research area and the objectives and methods of my study. In the discussion of methodology which follows, I focus upon positionality (the researcher's status relative to the researched in terms of characteristics such as class, race, culture, politics and power); the conducting of interviews; questionnaire design and implementation; participant observation; and data accessibility and accuracy. There is considerable literature on research methods, and a selection of useful references is to be found at the end of this chapter and in Chapter 13 of this monograph. I would strongly advise taking a field methods book with you, and referring to it as you go along. However much forward planning you do, your field methods will depend on the (often unforeseen) circumstances encountered in the field, and the ability to double-check your approach at each stage will be invaluable.

RESEARCH CONTEXT

In 1987, after a prolonged armed struggle against a resistance movement spearheaded by the Miskitu Indians, Nicaragua's revolutionary Sandinista government ratified the Autonomy Statute. This statute recognised the cultural and territorial rights of the peoples of the Atlantic (Caribbean) Coast and gave them the right to self-government under two Autonomous Regional Councils.

I arrived in Nicaragua in July 1990, just after the Sandinistas had been defeated at election by the United Nicaraguan Opposition (UNO) coalition and the very first Autonomous Regional Councils, in the North

---

[1] This is an updated version of the chapter published in the first edition. References have been added and there are some qualifications to earlier advice. However, it is still, in essence, based on my own experiences and what I did at the time of my doctoral research.

and the South of the Atlantic Coast, had been elected. I was carrying out research for my doctoral thesis into the process of establishing regional self-government in the North Atlantic Autonomous Region (RAAN). My focus was upon the relationships between self-determination, land rights, indigenous cultural practices of land and resource use, environment and economic development in the RAAN. I was attempting to assess the possibilities of achieving long-term, sustainable economic development in the agricultural and forestry sectors of the RAAN, by and for the benefit of the peoples of the region, and taking into account their cultural practices. I was principally concerned with the Miskitu, who are the largest of the four ethnic groups inhabiting the RAAN.

The research drew on a number of data sources, including historical documents, statistics and reports from governmental and non-governmental institutions in Nicaragua, secondary literature, and the media (British, North American and Nicaraguan newspapers and Nicaraguan radio broadcasts). I also interviewed a range of people including Nicaraguan government ministers, political leaders, personnel of governmental and non-governmental organisations, religious and community leaders, and ordinary people. I carried out detailed studies in three Miskitu communities which involved conducting censuses, questionnaire surveys and informal interviews, as well as participant observation. Most of the interviews were carried out in either Spanish or Miskitu. By the time I went to the Miskitu communities I had a good grasp of Spanish and had learned some Miskitu, but I relied on the help of a local translator in two of the Miskitu study villages where little Spanish was spoken.

POSITIONALITY

Positionality profoundly affects all aspects of research which involve interaction with other people, especially when researching the lives of people of a different class, race and culture from the researcher - what is referred to as researching 'the other'. The personal characteristics of the researcher (such as race, gender, nationality, language use, class and political stance) can place the researcher in a position of power vis-à-vis the person or group being researched. This is particularly true in the case of a person from the 'First World' conducting research in the 'Third World', and can be accentuated if the country being researched was a former colony of the researcher's country of origin (Madge, 1993; Sidaway, 1992).

Historically, Nicaragua's Atlantic Coast has been subject to the cultural and economic hegemony of white anglophones (predominantly from Britain and the USA), who have inculcated into the local population a respect for, and deference to, people with these characteristics. There is a tendency for such people to be perceived to be powerful and even superior. Thus, in some ways, for a British or US researcher on the Atlantic Coast, the relationship between the researcher and the researched is a continuation of the relationship between coloniser and colonised.

I found, like my predecessor Charles Hale (1989) (whose Ph.D. thesis concerned the Miskitu in the Southern Atlantic Coast), that being a white anglophone was useful in gaining acceptance on the Atlantic Coast. Because of the historical antagonisms between the peoples of the Atlantic Coast and the representatives of the Nicaraguan state, who are predominantly Mestizos (Spanish speakers of mixed indigenous and European descent), I would probably have been less well received had I been a Mestizo person, especially if I had been from Pacific Nicaragua.

However, the unequal power relationship between researcher and researched can have negative consequences for fieldwork. A common problem in conducting field research is the tendency for respondents to tell the researcher what they believe she or he wants to hear, especially when there is a marked power inequality between researcher and researched. Another problem is that the very presence of the researcher, by virtue of respondents' perceptions of his or her being a powerful person, can generate a whole host of expectations on the part of the respondents. This was particularly true in my case, because of the situation of the Atlantic Coast at the time of the research.

The region had just emerged from almost ten years of war, and towards the end of that period many westerners who visited the region were representatives of non-governmental organisations (NGOs) whose enquiries were directed towards the provision of aid. Consequently, my research was perceived as being part of an aid project. Much as I tried to convince villagers that my study was purely academic, many clung to the belief that I would be able to change their situation.[2] Respondents believed that I would be able to present my findings in person to the British Prime Minister, who would then ensure that help would be directed to their communities. Although I tried to explain that this was unlikely, for much of my research I felt rather a fraud, and also rather guilty that, in fact, I was doing 'merely' an academic study. Moreover, I found that my good intentions about actively using my research to draw attention to the needs of the country of study were overtaken by pressures to meet academic deadlines, and the hefty cost of making copies of the thesis. In most cases, however well-meaning, it is the researcher who really benefits from the research. The research participants, if they are lucky, will benefit only in the very long term from policy changes which may be brought about as a

---

[2] Elsbeth Robson & Uwem Ite also comment on this in their contributions.

result of the research. It is as well to bear this in mind, in terms of being realistic about what can be achieved by an individual research student, and in terms of trying to think ahead about how the research can promote the interests of the people being studied. Moreover, it is important to do the utmost to avoid generating false expectations.

On a more positive note, affiliation with a development organisation in the country of research, or in the researcher's own country, can improve the prospects of the work serving a useful purpose for the people being studied.[3] One way to begin repaying the debt to the country where the research was carried out is to send a copy of your thesis or dissertation to the institution(s) which supported the work. However, this still restricts access to your work, because only those who speak your language will be able to read it. Ideally, your findings need to be made available in at least the national language, and preferably (although this is much more difficult to organise) the local language. This can be achieved by publishing your work in a magazine or journal in the country where the research was undertaken, or sending reports of your findings to institutions and communities which supported your work (see Porter, 1995; Potter, 1993; Sidaway, 1993). I did manage to send copies of my thesis to the main institutions which supported my work, and I published my results in a Nicaraguan publication which specialises in Atlantic Coast issues and publishes in the languages of the Coast. I also presented aspects of my work to NGO personnel and invited local government officials in Puerto Cabezas. However, besides returning my census results, unfortunately I did not submit any written material to the study communities, due to time and money constraints.

Another aspect of the perception of the researcher as a powerful and influential person, is the belief that he or she is very affluent. Certainly in relation to the people being researched this is often the case, but even so there is only so much that can be done with a research budget. I felt rather awkward when almost every household that I visited during my questionnaire survey presented me with a gift and I felt that I should give something in return. I soon found that items such as aspirins were scarce and highly appreciated, while certain foodstuffs such as refined sugar and wheat flour, which people did not produce themselves, were also in demand. I tended to keep a small stock of such items to give to people who requested them. I am now more aware of the problems of handing out medicines, and would urge great caution in this respect. Besides the inconvenience of becoming regarded as a walking dispensary, there is the

---

[3] See Simon Batterbury's contribution for a more detailed discussion of institutional affiliation.

danger that cheap, effective, traditional remedies will be undermined by this practice, while people who really need to see a doctor do not go because they think that your medicine will cure them. Moreover, dispensing even a simple remedy for the wrong condition can be dangerous. Although in many countries all manner of medicines are available over the counter, I would now try to avoid dispensing medicine and stick to basic first aid and helping to get the patient to a doctor.

'An object of interest - For weeks Bob, the budding ecologist, thought he was minutely recording the nocturnal habits of the lesser spotted warthog, but in fact it was the local kids watching him!'

I tended to give gifts to people with whom I had stayed, or who had been particularly helpful to me, and chose to reciprocate towards families who had participated in the survey in the village where I had spent the most time, by taking their photographs. This was not without its problems. Everyone in the village wanted their photograph taken and many villagers took offence when I limited the photographs to those who had participated in the survey. Because of the commotion caused every time I produced my camera, I decided to take all the pictures on one day, and I found myself, like the pied piper of Hamlyn, being followed around the village by crowds of children shouting '*Miriki, miriki, Lilk ai kum alks!*' (which means 'American, American, take my picture!').[4] Clearly, affluent foreigners are expected to be generous, but there is a need to be discriminating, to find small but valued ways to reciprocate on a daily basis and be prepared to give larger gifts and provide emergency money on special occasions.

A practical implication of respondents' perceptions of the researcher's agenda is that the expectations of aid following the study can influence the research results. People may portray their situation in the worst possible light to maximise the possibility of receiving aid. For example, respondents may deliberately underestimate crop yields, or claim to own no agricultural tools. For people who are indeed in extremely difficult economic circumstances, this is a form of survival strategy, and is a scenario that the researcher should be aware of. I found it useful to double check (discretely!) with my close contacts in the villages results that seemed rather dubious. I found much of my data on agricultural and forestry practices very useful for establishing general trends in agriculture and forestry in the communities, and my findings generally conformed to regional patterns. However, because I suspected that there were some inaccuracies and inconsistencies, I decided that it would not be meaningful to subject the data to sophisticated statistical analysis. Moreover, some of the most uncertain material was excluded from analysis.

Political position
The actual or perceived political affiliation of the researcher also has an important bearing on the outcome of research. This is especially true in Nicaragua, since it is a country of bitter political divisions. At the time of the research there was a profound political polarisation between supporters of the Sandinistas and supporters of their opponents, including former counter-revolutionary resistance fighters (*Contras*). On the Atlantic Coast, these divisions were further complicated by political cleavages along ethnic lines, with the opposition to the Sandinistas divided into predominantly Mestizo supporters of the UNO and indigenous supporters of the YATAMA (Indian resistance) movement. Most foreigners visiting Nicaragua during the eighties were either working in solidarity with the revolution, or operating as undercover agents for the counter-revolutionaries. Consequently, as a foreigner, I was perceived as having either one of these political agendas.

---

[4] Elsbeth Robson discusses issues surrounding taking photographs during fieldwork in her chapter. See also Ellen (1984).

Because I wanted to interview people from across the political spectrum, I was anxious to avoid being labelled as belonging to one camp or another, in case this might make certain people reluctant to talk to me. I therefore had to consider carefully my affiliations within Nicaragua. From a practical point of view, having never visited Nicaragua before, affiliation with a local organisation was crucial since this would provide me with a base; the use of facilities such as libraries, computers, and telephones (which are otherwise difficult to gain access to); and the opportunity to liaise with Nicaraguan researchers.

I decided to affiliate to the Centre for Investigation and Documentation of the Atlantic Coast (CIDCA), since it was the only institute dedicated to research on the Atlantic Coast and has an international reputation. However, the organisation is strongly identified with the Sandinistas, having grown out of the former government ministry for the Atlantic Coast. This was very useful when I needed to make contact with Sandinista politicians and organisers, but meant that I had to play down my links with the organisation when interviewing opponents of the Sandinistas. However, Puerto Cabezas, the main town of the RAAN, is small and it was impossible to gloss over my links with CIDCA (not least because the YATAMA office was within a stone's throw of the CIDCA office!). Consequently, I was open about my links with CIDCA and made a point of stressing the practical reasons for my affiliation, which was usually accepted. Fortunately, the relationship between CIDCA and YATAMA in Puerto Cabezas was reasonably good.

I was, in fact, in a rather contradictory political position, being broadly supportive of the goals of the Sandinista revolution (although at times critical of the means used to achieve them), while also being strongly sympathetic to the indigenous struggle. This contradictory position, which is also discussed by Hale (1989, 1994), meant that I could have fallen foul of either side, although for the most part I managed to avoid such problems. In fact, during the course of the fieldwork, there was some rapprochement between elements of YATAMA and the Sandinistas. In all, probably the best way to minimise political problems is to be keenly aware of the political position of the people with whom you are interacting, and be very careful about the political signals that you, as a researcher, may be sending.

Another potential problem in conducting research in a highly politically charged situation is that people may be reluctant to be interviewed or unwilling to state their opinions. What I found to be more common was that people were keen to be interviewed because they wanted to make a political point. Consequently, it was important to be aware of where people were located within the complex network of political affiliations in order to attempt to evaluate the evidence they provided. This also applied to the examination of media sources. Although it is impossible to arrive at an objective account of a situation, through an awareness of the political positionality of sources it is possible to make a more plausible interpretation of evidence, and to identify the different discourses on a particular topic.

Finally, when conducting research in a politically or otherwise sensitive situation, it is often necessary to protect the anonymity of informants. General issues of confidentiality are discussed by Burgess (1994, Chapter 9), while Hale's work (1989, 1994) provides insights into the problems of work in politically volatile contexts. In such situations it is important to take every possible step to avoid informants being identified, which can extend to concealing the identities of respondents and even settlements in field notes, if there is a danger of them receiving unwanted attention.

Gender[5]

In societies where there is a strict division of gender roles, the gender of the researcher can severely restrict access to certain informants or situations. In my research this was not a particular problem, partly because my status as an outsider placed me somewhat outside the normal gender division of activities, and also because of the nature of the society within which I was working. Although Nicaraguan women (especially on the Atlantic Coast) have less economic and political power than men, may do less work outside the domestic sphere, and generally stay at home while the men go out drinking, they are by no means excluded from economic and political power, nor from the public domain. The Moravian faith, which is dominant among the Miskitu, forbids drinking and dancing and requires a strict moral code of behaviour from women. However, not all Coast people are Moravians, and many do not abide by its strictures once they are in the main town.

One of the places that I found very useful for informal information gathering and tuning into 'men's talk', was the bar. When stranded in small townships waiting for an onward boat or truck while travelling alone or at weekends, there was not much else to do. Invariably, I found minor political officials and NGO workers settled in for an afternoon session, often engaging in what I found to be very interesting conversations about local issues. Although women did go into bars in the main towns, it was unusual to find women alone in such places. Because women tend not to

---

[5] Gender roles in field research and their importance in the context of Nigeria are also discussed in Chapter 4.

have their own incomes, they are dependent on a man to take them out, and often vulnerable to being taken advantage of as a result. Despite experiencing some awkward moments while 'trespassing' alone into male-dominated realms, I did not encounter any major problems and on some occasions found myself drawn into fascinating conversations.

The gender of the researcher and the respondents can influence the types of information that can be obtained. For example, a female researcher may achieve a better rapport with a female respondent than could be achieved by a male researcher, and she might therefore be privy to more information, of a more personal nature, than he would. In fact, in some societies customs of female seclusion would make it very difficult indeed for a man to interview women. In a society where politics is very much a male preserve, a female researcher may not gain as much information as a male researcher on political issues. However, the advantage of being a woman is that you are less likely to be regarded as a political threat as you are probably less likely to be perceived as some kind of spy or undercover agent, for example. Consequently, men may be less guarded when talking to you about political issues than they might be with a male researcher. Having said this, for much of my work in the communities I was communicating through a male interpreter and so my gender probably had less impact on the research than it might have done.

It is hard to say how much easier or harder it would have been to carry out my research if I had been a man. I do not know whether part of the reason why complete strangers were so hospitable and helpful to me was because I was a woman and they felt in some way protective towards me, or whether it was a reflection of the hospitality of the Nicaraguan people. I suspect the latter.

I did, however, find that there were significant disadvantages to being a woman, especially when interviewing certain men. However professional you might wish to appear (and when you are doing your very first piece of overseas fieldwork, you may not feel very confident or professional), your research mission may be of far less relevance to respondents than your status as a woman. Dressing smartly and formally as well as carrying business cards can greatly enhance your professional image. Nevertheless, it pays to be aware of the potential pitfalls of agreeing to meet interviewees, however formal and businesslike they might appear to be, outside of office hours or in informal situations (for example in bars or restaurants). In the case of people who are clearly very busy during working hours, this kind of arrangement seems a practical solution, but on occasion might lead to embarrassing or awkward situations.

PRACTICALITIES OF INTERVIEWING

The last point raises a number of practical issues concerning interviews in informal situations (see also Burgess, 1984; Ellen, 1984). While such interviews can provide the most intriguing information, it can also be more difficult to record information in such situations without prejudicing the flow of conversation (respondents may be less open if they see you taking notes). In these situations it is better to try to remember as much as possible at the time and write it down at the first opportunity after the interview. How much of this material you decide to submit to print, and whether you name sources, is a matter for your conscience.

Another issue is **when** to interview people. There are bound to be key informants, such as prominent political leaders or government ministers, whose input to the study is regarded as crucial. These people are often elusive and very busy. On the one hand, it pays to contact such informants at the earliest possible stage to ensure that there will be a chance of talking to them. This may require writing to them in the first instance, to introduce yourself and request an appointment, followed by a call or a visit to their office to speak to their secretary. Patience and persistence are crucial in such cases - do not be surprised to find that even when you have a formal appointment, you do not necessarily get to the see the person concerned on the first visit.

On the other hand, there is a lot to be said for waiting until you have gained a full grasp of the local language and the issues at stake before approaching key informants. You will then be in a position to pose more pertinent and penetrating questions and maximise the information gained from the interview. I tried to interview key people almost as soon as I arrived, but with hindsight, I would have done better to have left those interviews until I had spent more time in Nicaragua.

A common dilemma is whether or not to tape record interviews. On the one hand, taping allows the researcher to concentrate on the conversation and replay important parts of the interview at leisure, as well as to extract verbatim quotes. Moreover, if the researcher has yet to master the language of the country, taping means that important information will not be lost through lack of understanding. On the other hand, people may be less open if they know that they are being tape recorded, and the transcription of tapes is a painfully slow business. If interviews are taped, they should be transcribed as soon as possible afterwards. It goes without saying that permission should always be asked before tape recording an interview. After the initial two or three months, I limited my recordings to interviews with key informants and meetings where Miskitu was the main language spoken.

QUESTIONNAIRE DESIGN

In this section I include a number of points which are widely addressed in the existing literature on research design and are not specific to research overseas. The first point concerns questionnaire design. Moser and Kalton (1979, pp. 303-349) raise general issues concerning questionnaire design, while Harris (1984) provides a useful guide when designing questionnaires about rural economies in developing countries. Ideally, a draft questionnaire should be prepared prior to the field visit. However, it may be necessary to modify the original draft substantially to account for possible changes in research direction and in the light of gaining a fuller understanding of local conditions. This was true in my case; in fact it was not until I had spent a few months in the field that my research objectives really became focused. When re-drafting the questionnaire, I would strongly advise seeking help from personnel of government ministries, NGOs and research institutes, since these people can give detailed advice about the conditions you are likely to encounter in your study area and provide constructive criticism of your questionnaire. It is also crucial to acquaint yourself with the local system of weights and measures, which may well differ from national or international standard measures. Finally, wherever possible, a pilot survey should be carried out in order to highlight areas of ambiguity, or where further questions may be useful. The sample size of the pilot survey depends upon the time and money available, and the size of the final sample. Ideally, it should enable you to capture as wide a range of responses to the questions as possible. However, even a relatively small survey (perhaps ten respondents) can provide valuable feedback. Ideally, the method of sampling should follow that intended for the final survey, in order to test the sampling technique.

QUESTIONNAIRE IMPLEMENTATION

I carried out questionnaire surveys with members of households selected randomly from each of three study villages. Because there were no census data available, I decided to carry out my own census of each of the villages prior to selecting households for survey. This provided a picture of the social and economic characteristics of the villages, as well as giving me the opportunity to introduce myself to the inhabitants of the villages. In the process of conducting the censuses I mapped and numbered the dwellings in each village. The maps were divided into grid squares and dwellings (which in most cases corresponded to households) were selected for study by picking numbers from a table of random numbers and matching these to co-ordinates on the grid. I found this method very slow because, owing to the way in which houses were scattered unevenly within the settlements, it took many attempts to find numbers that corresponded to dwellings. I discovered that a less painstaking way of selecting households for study was by the 'lottery method' (Moser & Kalton, 1979, p. 82). I wrote the number of each dwelling on a piece of paper, folded all the pieces, put them in a box and picked them out at random, as in a raffle. Where more than one household shared a dwelling, they each received a separate letter as well as the number. This avoided the problem of how to decide which households to interview where more than one household lived in the same house. However, it pays to find out as much as possible about the relationships between households living in the same dwelling.

I defined households as comprising a group of people who live in the same dwelling, cook together, and pool their resources. In reality, households rarely form discrete economic units, since many households rely on contributions from extended family members within the village, in other settlements or even living abroad. Moreover, the household is not a static unit, since some household members spend part of the year working outside the village. In my study I included people who were expected to return to the live in the household for part of the year, but excluded people who had been absent for an extended period of time, or when there was uncertainty about their return. Despite these limitations, the household provided a point of departure for examining the village economy and a manageable unit for sampling.

There are a number of different approaches to sampling depending to some extent on the nature, size and distribution of the population to be sampled. If the population is large and diverse and you wish to ensure balanced representation of key sub-groups within that population (for example, different social classes) then a stratified sample may be appropriate. This means that the sample frame is subdivided and separate samples are taken from each of the key strata within the population. If the only data available are in the form of settlement maps and the settlement is too large to enumerate yourself, a form of multi-stage sampling can be carried out. The map is divided into blocks, the blocks are numbered and a number of blocks randomly chosen. The selected blocks can then be enumerated or mapped and samples chosen from them (Moser & Kalton, 1979, 118-119).Whichever method is chosen, it is important to remember that if you want to be able to use statistics for inference about the entire population, the sample must be randomly chosen, and representative of the population as a whole.

Sample size can be another difficulty. I found that although I had interviewed representatives from over half of the households in the villages, and in all but one case had over fifty respondent households, I still did not have a large enough sample to carry out statistical tests such as chi square to make comparisons between the villages. Clearly it pays to get as big a sample as possible if statistical analysis between sub-samples is desired. I resolved the problem of inadequate sample size by using the less rigorous standard error test for statistical significance, which can found in any statistics text book.

My next set of points bear more directly upon issues of conducting questionnaires in an overseas context, and relate to the use of interpreters. Clearly, the problem of misunderstandings are minimised if both interviewer and interviewee have a common first language. The next best thing is to try to communicate directly in the interviewee's language, or for the interviewee to speak your language. However, at times the need for an interpreter is unavoidable. The only way to minimise the inaccuracies involved with communicating through a third person is to have at least a basic understanding of the language concerned and the key words required for your work, so that you can get some idea of whether your questions are being asked in the way you intended. It also pays to keep the questions as simple and straightforward as possible when there is a language barrier.[6]

Initially it took an hour and a half or more to complete each questionnaire, but over time, as myself and my interpreter learned how best to ask the questions, I found that we could complete a questionnaire session in about three-quarters of an hour. Working all day we could complete six or seven questionnaires, but often we only carried out four and conducted informal interviews during the afternoon. It is always important to allow plenty of time for questionnaire surveys, because it will take time to walk around the settlements, and invariably people will not be at home on the first visit, or they may not wish to participate in the study. If you are collecting agricultural data, try to avoid very busy times of the agricultural year - farmers may be out in the field from dawn to dark.

An associated issue is whether to employ an interpreter from the study village, or an outsider.[7] The advantage of an outsider is that she or he is unlikely to be involved in any disputes within the village and is likely to be regarded as neutral. Originally, CIDCA found a translator for me from Puerto Cabezas. However, she had other commitments and was not always able to come to work in the village. Luckily, the family with whom I stayed when I was in Puerto Cabezas had a relative in one of my study villages who offered to work for me as an interpreter. One of the issues that I was researching was a conflict over land between the interpreters' village and the neighbouring village, and I was concerned that his presence

---

[6] See also Elsbeth Robson's chapter. Ellen (1984) makes useful comments on working in a foreign language and the use of field assistants, while Smith (1996) and Western (1996) discuss the problems of interpretation or research exchanges carried out in a different language.

[7] Employing translators/research assistants is further discussed in Chapter 4.

would prejudice the outcome of the research. However, luckily, some of the interviewees in the rival village were relatives of his, some were unaware that he was from the other village, and no one appeared too reticent about telling us what they thought about the issue. I found that it was a great advantage to employ a local translator, not least because he was permanently based in the village. His familiarity with local residents facilitated organising interviews and helped me to gain acceptance in the village and he knew all the local idiosyncrasies and the names of the various places where people grew crops and had land.[8]

Besides the support of the local interpreter, my acceptance in the more traditional of the villages was also contingent upon my being sanctioned by the Moravian pastor, who was regarded as a pillar of society in that particular village. It therefore pays to identify the person or persons who wield influence in the community ('gatekeepers') and seek their approval before embarking on fieldwork.[9]

PARTICIPANT OBSERVATION
Participant observation is the process of collecting data from observations made during the course of participating in the everyday affairs of the research subjects. I found this approach extremely valuable in my research. During interviews and questionnaire surveys the information offered to the researcher is largely determined by the questions the researcher chooses to ask, whereas participant observation can reveal information about important issues of which the researcher was unaware, or about which he or she had not thought to ask. Participant observation can also provide information in its appropriate context, rather than in artificially engineered settings such as during a survey, and insight into the various accounts of a situation given by different social actors, expressed in their own language.

Throughout my research I recorded in my field notebooks any information that I thought might be of interest, derived from my observations of events and from conversations. As part of the strategy of participant observation, I made a point of attending community meetings, church services and social gatherings, especially during my visits to the study communities. Such observations complemented the data gained during the more formal interviews and also generated ideas for further areas of investigation. During the work in the study communities where little Spanish was spoken, I relied on my interpreter to explain to me what was going on during community gatherings.

---

[8] See Chapter 4 for a discussion of rates of pay for translators.
[9] See also Burgess (1984, pp. 48-49; pp. 194-197).

While there is a lot to be gained from the 'fly on the wall' approach, it is important that the researcher remembers that he or she is by no means an invisible fly and her or his presence may well alter the nature of the interactions being observed. As mentioned earlier, the researcher needs to be aware that she or he is likely to be judged by the company they keep and this can affect relationships with other people. Although the tendency for people to modify their behaviour in the presence of the researcher is less likely to occur if the people being observed are not aware that the researcher is recording their actions, the ethics of covertly observing people without their knowledge are extremely questionable. In fact, even if people are aware that you are studying their community, they may be rather alarmed at quite how much detail you are recording. Although detailed personal information can be very revealing and useful, the researcher should think carefully about how such material should be recorded and used.[10] Finally, even when the researcher is attempting to observe passively and not impose a preconceived structure on data, the data gained from participant observation are still influenced by the researcher's own perceptions.

DATA AVAILABILITY AND ACCURACY

The difficulties of collecting data on household incomes are well known - people the world over are generally reluctant to discuss how much money they make. Besides this obvious difficulty, I also encountered problems in collecting data on crop yields, since villagers did not always measure their crop yields. This was especially true of root crops, which are harvested incrementally as they are required for household use. Consequently, much of my crop yield data could only be used as a rough indicator of the state of the agricultural economy.

A further source of potential inaccuracy in data collection arises if the researcher unwittingly suggests to respondents the anticipated answer to a particular question. Care must therefore be taken to pose questions in a neutral and open manner, so as not to pre-empt the response. For example, it was better to ask respondents what they thought the main reasons were for the war (between the Miskitus and the Sandinistas) than to ask whether land was the main reason. The first case may provoke a variety of responses, whereas in the second case the question is answered simply 'yes' or 'no' or 'don't know'. However, the collection and processing of data is easier if the researcher has outlined the possible responses to a particular question on the questionnaire and merely ticks a box to record the answer. It is useful to leave enough space for additional

---

[10] Clare Madge discusses the ethics of participant observation in her chapter.

information, or for responses that do not conform to the anticipated possibilities, which should be recorded in full.

Despite time pressures, it is not only fair, but also useful, to chat informally to the respondents after the questionnaire has been completed, if they want to do so. In this way, the interview process is not simply a one-way flow of information, but enables the respondents to find out about the researcher and his or her work. Moreover, respondents may state opinions, or provide information, during informal conversations which they did not volunteer during the formal questionnaire session. Whether it is ethical to use such information to supplement questionnaire data is debatable and depends on the kind of information being given and the extent to which the person felt that they were telling you the information 'off the record'. I tended to use the information if it was volunteered spontaneously, although I generally avoided giving respondents' names in the write up of the data.

Data quality can be influenced by storytelling and popular mythology, and therefore accounts should not always be taken at face value. Respondents may embellish accounts to portray themselves or their people in the best possible light, and employ poetic license. One aspect of this is the portrayal of the past as being far rosier than the present. This is not unique to the Nicaraguan Miskitu, but in their case the dramatic events of the last decade give them more cause than most to hark back to a former golden era. Villagers may exaggerate just how much better life was in the past, which can mislead the researcher. For example, many of my respondents claimed that before the Sandinistas came, everyone in their village had large numbers of cattle, whereas according to my close contacts within the villages and also in the government agricultural ministry, most people had only a few cattle and some had none. This is another reason to employ a local translator, since he or she is better equipped than the researcher to spot inaccuracies, or tall stories.

However, it is impossible for researchers to do what Haraway (1988) describes as 'the god-trick' - to situate themselves outside of the research in order to view issues totally objectively. As we have already seen, the researcher is inextricably bound within a cultural identity and set of power relations, such that she or he cannot enter the field as a completely neutral observer. Field observations and data pass through the prism of the prejudices, values and ideals of both researcher and researched.

It can prove as difficult to find objective data from written documents as from verbal accounts, since, for example, data from different government sources may prove contradictory. Moreover, 'Third World' government institutions commonly lack the resources to collect social and economic data, or are hampered by war. I could not find many documents concerning the regional economy, because they had been destroyed, lost or misplaced during the upheavals of the war and re-shuffling of government ministries. When documents are finally unearthed, there may be no quick way to copy them because of the scarcity of photocopying facilities. I spent many afternoons painstakingly copying data from government reports by hand. Needless to say, it is advisable to read carefully over any tables and lists of figures that are hand copied before leaving the office.

This last point brings me to a more general piece of advice about data collection in the field - meticulous documentation and filing of material in the field is worth many hours of frustration at the time of writing up. Careful records of all interviews should be kept, including the full names and offices of the persons involved and the dates and places of the interviews. An index of the contents of field notebooks with page numbers should be continuously updated. I found that exercise books were far easier to use than reporters' notebooks. It is also crucial to review records frequently while in the field, to enable identification of patterns and to highlight areas where more data are required. As noted above, transcription of tape-recorded interviews should be carried out as soon as possible after they are conducted. If possible, the coding of questionnaires for statistical analysis can also be carried out in the field, although it is advisable to wait until most questionnaires are complete before devising a coding system. A prior knowledge of the computer statistical package to be used in analysis is useful in this respect. However, I would advise tackling the analysis of data in stages, as and when it is needed for each part of the thesis. This prevents the researcher using data analysis as a means to postpone the writing stage, which can be psychologically the hardest part of the work. Analysing the data as they are required also ensures that analysis is directly relevant to the points being made and helps avoid wasting time and effort.

USING PHOTOGRAPHS IN RESEARCH

Taking photographs is often part of fieldwork and can provide another form of data. However, it is an activity with many ethical considerations and requires contemplation of the way in which you will use photographs in your own research. Images are powerful and often very personal. You have to make choices about what to photograph and, later on, which photographs to use and how. Photography can be intrusive, an objectification of the research subject. It goes without saying that, as far as possible, you should ask permission before photographing people. One of the problems is that this then interrupts whatever activity it is that you wanted to photograph, detracting from its spontaneity. Moreover, people often do not like to be photographed in their work clothes, nor their children to be photographed in their everyday state (often wearing old clothes, or semi-clad). To fail to respect this is a violation of people's dignity, but this may mean that the photographs you do take are not really representative of day-to-day life. Another consideration is whether your pictures are 'accurate', whether they overrepresent or underrepresent certain groups, and whether your editing and use of then distorts the 'reality' that you are trying to portray. It is worth making an effort to record the identity and context of the pictures at the time, rather than relying solely on memory.

CONCLUSION

As this discussion shows there is no perfect formula for carrying out fieldwork overseas. In hindsight, I have suggested how to avoid some common pitfalls. However, there are a number of issues concerning reciprocity, ethics and the whole question of whether privileged researchers from the 'First World' should engage in research in impoverished 'Third World' countries which are less easy to resolve.[11] What I am sure about is that I would not have been able to complete my fieldwork without the help of a great many people in Nicaragua, and I would like to take this opportunity to thank them. I would like to dedicate this chapter to the memory of Felix Lampson Ignacio.

REFERENCES

Burgess, Robert C. 1984 <u>In the Field: An Introduction to Field Research</u> London: Allen and Unwin.

Ellen, R.F. (ed) 1984 <u>Ethnographic Research: A Guide to General Conduct</u> London: Academic Press.

Hale, Charles 1989 <u>Contradictory consciousness: Miskitu Indians and the Nicaraguan state in conflict and reconciliation (1860-1987)</u> Unpublished Ph.D. Thesis, Stanford University.

Hale, Charles 1994 <u>Resistance and Contradiction: Miskitu Indians and the Nicaraguan State, 1894-1987</u> Stanford: Stanford University Press.

Haraway, Donna 1988 'Situated knowledges: the science question in feminism and the privilege of partial perspective' <u>Feminist Studies</u> 14, 3.

Harris, Barbara 1984 <u>Analysing the Rural Economy</u> University of East Anglia, Discussion Paper No. 164.

---

[11] These ethical questions are dealt with further in chapter 7.

Madge, Clare 1993 'Boundary disputes: Comments on Sidaway (1992)', Area 25, 3, 294-299.

Moser, Claus A. & Graham Kalton 1979 Survey Methods in Social Investigation Aldershot: Gower.

Porter, Gina 1995 '"Third World" research by "First World" geographers: An Africanist perspective', Area 27, 2, 139-141.

Potter, Robert 1993 'Little England and little geography: Reflections on Third World teaching and research', Area 25, 3, 291-194.

Sidaway, James 1992 'In other worlds: On the politics of research by "First World" geographers in the "Third World"', Area 24, 4, 403-408.

Smith, Fiona 1996 'Problematising language: Limitations and possibilities in "foreign language" research', Area 28, 2, 160-166.

Western, John 1996 'Qualitative research and the language trap', Area 28, 2, 235-238.

3.

FLEXIBILITY, FUNDING AND FORESIGHT: TIPS FOR THE PHYSICAL GEOGRAPHER IN DEVELOPING AREAS RESEARCH

Georgina H. Endfield and Peter W. O'Connor

INTRODUCTION
Undertaking fieldwork abroad presents one the most challenging and memorable experiences for the geographer, whatever the nature of the project he or she is undertaking. Practical tips for physical geography fieldworkers overseas, along with the logistical problems they might face in developing countries, vary little from those of their human geography cousins, though there are certain additional issues that scientific project workers should perhaps consider. These specific issues are rarely discussed in the literature. Here we propose to deal with some of those issues, though the reader is directed to other sections of this monograph, dealing with more general fieldwork guidelines. We draw largely on our own experiences carrying out overseas fieldwork. Peter spent two months (July-August, 1995) in southern Africa undertaking research for his Ph.D. on climatic change, and establishing the former extent of the Kalahari Desert. Georgina carried out her research in central Mexico, over a nine month period (September 1995-May 1996) investigating environmental change since the Spanish Conquest through archival and documentary media and field evidence.

FUNDING FOR PHYSICAL GEOGRAPHY FIELDWORK
Conducting research in developing areas can be a costly business. This is especially true when the project involves working in isolated locations and just reaching your research area can impose a large financial burden. Flights and travel costs will inevitably consume a large portion of the research budget. In some countries the exchange rate may work in your favour such that the grant or sponsorship you are supported by (if indeed you are) back home may well prove sufficient to support you while you are away. With an average of eleven pesos to the pound, Georgina encountered few budgeting problems on a recent trip to Mexico. In other circumstances, however, where the cost of living may be disproportionately high, it is often necessary to seek funding from outside

your home institution. Loans are always an option, especially if a large amount of capital is to be invested in the purchase of a vehicle. It may be possible, for example, to arrange an interest-free loan with the backing and support of a university department as Chasca Twyman (Sheffield) did, enabling her to purchase a four wheel drive vehicle for her research in Botswana. Some general practical advice on how to go about fund raising is given in Chapter 1, and potential sources of financing are listed in Chapter 13: *Useful References*. The competition for funding, however, is intense, with a large number of people applying for a limited amount of money. It is advisable to target those funding bodies and institutions whose objectives most closely match the aims of your research, as often this course of action will reduce the number of applicants with whom you are competing. There are, for example, a number of research groups who have funds to support exclusively physical geography research, such as The British Geomorphological Research group and The Quaternary Research Association[1], while other funding bodies and trusts can be approached providing they support physical science projects. Identifying the most appropriate strategy and the most suitable organisations to approach before you plan your fieldwork can determine the viability of your project in the long run.

QUESTIONS, CONTACTS AND COUNSEL

Fieldwork in developing areas necessarily requires meticulous planning. Some of the most critical issues for the physical geographer include i) accessibility, both to equipment and sites in the field area, and ii) transportation of equipment and samples. If your supervisor does not have personal experience of the site area (which is often the case), it is important to contact someone who has. If possible, you should find out what type of facilities for analysis are available in the field, if any; what kind of equipment might be available in host institutions, and if there will be transportation to move it. Is there likely to be storage space for samples if they cannot all be returned home at the same time, and will there be facilities to keep them refrigerated if necessary?

"Landsat" imagery is most often a method for site selection, and may be the sole source of geomorphological information, especially in remote areas with poor map coverage. Here again, contact with someone who has first hand knowledge of the area can yield untold benefits in the form of advice, support and tips. Such sources may also prove invaluable from another perspective, as often institutions require letters of introduction or references before they will consider affiliation or a permit.

---

[1] Addresses in Chapter 13.

The name of a lecturer or a professor from a well-respected institution overseas can carry a lot of weight at a consulate, immigration or embassy office. Addresses for contacts can be found through references to journal articles, through the internet, or by contacting relevant research organisations, who list the research interests and contact addresses of their members.

If personal transport is essential for your fieldwork, you should be clear on what type of vehicle you need to get. Would a car be sufficient, or can the area only be accessed by four wheel drive vehicles? Perhaps more importantly, can you afford to purchase a vehicle, or is it more viable to hire one? Your chosen course of action will, of course, depend on the nature of your research, the length of time you aim to spend in the field and, perhaps more significantly, your financial resources, but it is essential to weigh up the various advantages and disadvantages of the options open to you.

OVERSEAS LINKS: ADVANTAGES BY ASSOCIATION

Establishing affiliation with an institution in the host country can bring untold rewards for the researcher. Not only is there an immediate point of contact, and the opportunity to interact with other people, perhaps even in the same position as yourself, but the additional possibility of making use of the resources that this affiliation has to offer. It may well be possible, for example, to become involved in an ongoing project, at least nominally, with all the benefits that this can bring. Access to photocopying, e-mail, fax and library facilities, and perhaps even a surrogate supervisor, are obvious advantages, but the availability of transport, certain pieces of equipment and access to laboratory facilities may add to the smooth running of your project while you are away. The "promise" of availability, however, does not necessarily bring with it an assurance of functionality, and even the best made research plans may all go horribly wrong when equipment is, at best, already in use, different to expectations, broken and in need of repair, or at worst, missing, stolen or non- existent. It is best to check, and then double check on the availability of equipment, or to make alternative plans to analyse materials at home should facilities be unavailable. The benefits of taking a reconnaissance trip to assess the situation cannot be overstated.

Extra funding opportunities with your host country may be more forthcoming if you can prove association with an institution or existing project, as the legitimacy of your presence becomes more obvious to the powers that be. It may well be worth exploring opportunities that may entitle you to certain monetary benefits such as exchange programmes, or government-sponsored schemes for physical or scientific projects. Be prepared, however, for long winded administrative application procedures given the sometimes seemingly unreasonable requirements for medical certificates, academic certification, student visas, research proposals, references (host and home country), photographs, curriculum vitae, copies of passports and migration papers. Moreover, funding can, of course, never be guaranteed. Economic downturns and political unrest in developing countries can lead to the withdrawal of promised grants, as recently happened in Mexico, where government sponsored CONACYT (Consejo Nacional de Ciencias y Tecnologia) overseas studentships were dramatically cut back, priority being given to domestic student projects. In preparing her trip to Mexico, for example, Georgina spent a good deal of time filling in forms and organising references for an application for one such grant, which was also being dealt with by the overseas institution to which she was affiliated. Upon arrival, however, all the paper work was abandoned as were the hopes of additional funding, given the cutbacks engendered by the economic disruption sweeping over the country at the time.

PERMIT ACQUISITION AND CUSTOMS

Physical geography research in developing areas usually involves large amounts of equipment and the removal of samples from your field area. This can add considerable bureaucratic problems to the organisation of a fieldwork period, usually requiring several months of organisation. When considering application for permits, you should have a good idea of what equipment your going to have to bring, as this may affect the nature of the permit you require. It may also be necessary to name on the permit individual items of equipment that look unusual, or might be perceived to have a negative effect on the environment. One researcher (Philip Rayn, Dublin City University), for example, using tracer dyes to follow the flow path of a river underground in Zimbabwe, received considerable local resistance to his project. Only after the production of a permit, describing the effects of the dye on the water supply, was the researcher in question allowed to continue with his work. A list of equipment might also be necessary for British or overseas customs. When passing through customs you should make sure to have, in addition to any permits, an official letter from your university and supervisor, preferably on headed notepaper, explaining what your doing, as simply and clearly as possible, and detailing the function of any unusual pieces of equipment. Some countries require a tax to be paid on pieces of equipment over a certain value, so you might also be required to list the value of some of your equipment.

Often when applying for permits it is necessary to provide some indication of the environmental impact your research will have. Such an assessment may need to be corroborated by an independent source, perhaps a researcher from an institution, usually from the host country. The inclusion of such information in the early stages of an application may speed the whole process on and help to reassure the country of research that your project will not have detrimental effect on the landscape or people.

The removal of samples from an area or country is sometimes forbidden and all countries will have some form of restriction to certain areas. It is important to find out at an early opportunity, exactly what these restrictions are. Usually in 'developing countries' those areas which have the greatest accessibility (e.g. National Parks) have the most restrictions imposed on them. Acquisition of permits for such areas usually involves contact with several departments and cannot be organised at the last minute.

Transporting samples across national boundaries may require a permit from the country you are entering as well as permits from the country from which you collected the samples. Having spent some time collecting his samples in Namibia, Peter faced problems crossing the border to Botswana. Unbeknown to him, there had been an outbreak of foot and mouth disease during his time in the field. As a result, border officials in Botswana wanted all his samples destroyed before entering the country. Luckily, the production of a permit from the office of the President in Botswana was sufficient to enable the border crossing.

ETHICS IN PHYSICAL GEOGRAPHY FIELDWORK

As with any foreign fieldworker in a developing country, the physical geographer needs to approach fieldwork with sensitivity and an awareness of local attitudes and customs.[2] Yet there are certain aspects of scientific fieldwork that demand special attention. Making an effort to speak the language or dialect of the host country is not only a human geography prerequisite, and can only add to your fieldwork experience. Being able to converse with local people not only facilitates the whole fieldwork procedure, but also serves to enhance the time you spend overseas. For many tourists, the answer would seem to lie in merely talking in their native tongue, but very loudly. Then there is the phrase book approach which can assist to a point, at least in dealing with basics such as accommodation and food supplies, but which is limited should you need to assess the quickest, safest bandit-free route to your fieldsite, or indeed should you have to consult a local head for permission to work and maybe camp at a particular site under their jurisdiction. Any attempt, however

---

[2] See Chapters by Elsbeth Robson, Uwem Ite and Clare Madge in this volume.

meagre, to speak the language does demonstrate respect for the host country. It is, moreover, not only human geographers who carry out interviews. Chatting in Spanish to some of the older members of a community was one of the ways in which Georgina was able to elicit information about the state of the landscapes, and the land use at the turn of the twentieth century in Mexico. One of the student's informants was also able to speak and read the ancient prehispanic language of the area and so was able to assist in the translation of some colonial land grant documents written in the native dialect. Being able to communicate with the local community can, therefore, bring an added facet to your research.

It is worthwhile approaching the community nearest to the area of your fieldwork before you start your fieldwork, to ensure permission to walk on their lands and, where necessary, to take samples from them. Affiliation to a group of local researchers working in the area, or indeed employing local labourers might, however, facilitate this, and reduce any animosity that might be felt. Local community heads in a small township in Michoacán, Mexico, for example, recently refused a team of American archaeologists permission to survey their lands. Admittedly, this could stem from the fact that a good proportion of their territory was sown with a splendid array of marijuana plants, but the obvious lack of indigenous consultation and involvement with the project on the part of the archaeologists went some way to consolidating this decision.

Some effort should be made to explain the purpose of the fieldwork, and more importantly from a physical geography perspective, to explain what the equipment you employ is used for. Lake-coring equipment, for example, can appear extremely threatening and noxious to a community accustomed to water shortage, and whose livelihood depends on the lake and its resources. While our aim as scientific researchers is to avoid any obvious changes to the landscape and environment, every effort should be made to restore any perceptible damage that is done.

Ultimately by carrying out foreign fieldwork, we take information from our host country, yet it is rare that the area of concern ever receives anything in return. Though not always applicable, some effort should be made to provide an institution within the host country with a copy of your finished research.

TIMING AND TIME MANAGEMENT
Deciding when to carry out fieldwork can almost be as important as planning what to do when you get there. Traveling on dirt roads during the rainy season can be almost impossible as well as dangerous, and "sleeping under the stars" can take on a whole new meaning when you wake to find your tent has been washed away in last night's freak rainstorm! Regardless

of the nature of your research, its essential to have an understanding of how climatic and environmental conditions will affect practical day to day living, accessibility to site areas, and the operation of your equipment. Will your Electronic Distance Meter fog up at 70% humidity? If you are bringing monitoring equipment, at what temperature ranges are levels of accuracy and precision affected?

Having decided on the most practical time to carry out fieldwork, the more crucial questions of practicality and feasibility should then be asked. Will the features you are interested in actually be there? What happens when after a year of fund raising and enthusiastic planning you go the Namib desert to measure sand dune movement and there's no wind? What will be your best strategy when you travel 8,000 miles to measure fluvial processes and there is no river because of drought during the previous six months? These situations are, unfortunately, all too common and should be seriously considered before you leave. It's important also to consider how environmental conditions prior to, and during your research will practically affect you and your equipment in meeting the aims of your research. Try and pick a time of year to travel in which the processes you are interested in are most likely to be operative.

Physical geography fieldwork can be often very labour intensive, restricting both the length of time you can spend in the field and how much you can realistically achieve. Your work may involve sampling, which usually involves lots of hole digging, a particularly draining task under "normal" conditions. If you are interested in losing weight, toning your body, developing a permanent back problem, or generally just going insane, we would personally recommend several months of this type of activity. If, however you are not overtly keen on such masochism, it would, perhaps, be wise to practise and plan ahead, and assess how much work you are capable of completing in a day considering the climatic conditions. This is a good basis on which to predict the length of time you need to spend in the field. It will also enable you to become familiar with your equipment and help you to decide whether you can really manage on your own.

The number of samples or the amount of data you need to collect and the length of time you spend in the field, is also determined by how much you can analyse upon your return. There is no point in spending extra time in the field collecting samples or field data, if you'll never have time to analyse them all. If it takes a week to collect enough data to keep you busy for the length of your research you might consider going home, though there is a lot to be said for further exploration and investigation of the country you are in. Take the opportunity to travel, make more contacts and perhaps even become involved in a local project that might add another facet to your work and that also "puts something back" into the area. You should, if at all possible, calculate how long the form of analysis relevant to you will take. This is most important if your sample analysis needs to be carried out in the host country for methodological reasons. Not only will this enable you to plan how long you need to stay, it also provides a framework in which the host institution can assess the feasibility of your proposal and the likelihood of them meeting your needs.

PURCHASING AND REPAIRS
Problems of accessing equipment, repairs, and the availability of, and access to suitable materials, calls for improvisation and it is at such times that the ingenuity of the individual is tested to the full. As would befit skills of the most able boy scout or girl guide, the physical geographer must be prepared to seek out substitute materials in the local haberdashery, iron-mongers, or employ the services of the local carpenter or metal worker. The demands of the physical geographer abroad, however, can bring local responses that range from mild amusement to complete disbelief. Afterall, what would a *gringo* possibly want with a 50 foot length of rope and 20 foot of reinforced steel piping? Clearly, there is something to be said for having some language skills in situations like this. Nevertheless, personal experience has shown the potential economic benefits of having equipment made out in the field, not to mention the savings made on luggage space and insurance costs, but it should be remembered that specifications will not be to standardised norms and this must be taken into account, or may unfortunately become disastrously apparent during fieldwork. Purchasing basic materials, such as sections of piping or plastic bags and containers for sediment storage, should present few problems provided there are suitable outlets that stock such merchandise, but the availability of specific chemicals for analysis is likely to be limited, at best, to major city areas. It is worthwhile checking availability before you leave home, and /or stocking up on supplies before you set out into the more remote areas of your host country. Moreover, it is important to enquire about airline regulations for chemical transportation should you want to bring specific materials with you.

PREPARING FOR THE UNEXPECTED
Carrying out physical geography fieldwork in developing areas can, and most probably will, throw a few unexpected punches. Generally the lack of previous research in these areas causes complications resulting from a reliance on out-of-date literature or data which have been gathered using less than ideal methods for your needs. The identification of landforms from satellite imagery and aerial photography can often be incorrect,

resulting in FPS (frustrated postgraduate syndrome) once in the field. Similarly, examples of landforms or potential sites for investigation may prove to be less than ideal once they are greeted in the flesh. It is important, therefore, to consider back-up plans before you leave, concerning both the location of your main site areas and adaptations to the overall aims of your research if conditions should dictate. During his time in southern Africa, for example, Peter O'Connor had to change his plans somewhat, shifting from field sites in Western Zambia to Northern Namibia, when the landforms he had hoped to investigate were in, effect, "missing" from the landscape. To expect everything not to go to plan is reasonable, but it should not present too much of a problem once you have taken the necessary time to collect your thoughts and make an alternative plan of action. The key is to avoid making rash or rushed decisions, as this may well result in even worse problems in the long run.

SALVATION UNDER SUFFERANCE: LOCAL CO-OPERATION IN FIELDWORK

Becoming part of a team of local investigators can be one of the most rewarding, yet frustrating, fieldwork experiences. Ultimately, there are the benefits of being integrated into a local research team who probably know more about the area than you can ever hope to. The team can assist in the logistical and practical aspects of your project, providing transport, equipment, storage and advice. Locals might also be able to gain access to areas where foreigners might not be so well received. In payment for all these benefits, however, certain aspects of your carefully pre-planned, time-managed fieldwork will inevitably be sacrificed. An acceptance that your schedule will be somewhat modified (on a scale ranging from "slight change" to "chaotic upheaval"), and an awareness of the need for flexibility can, however, ensure that, frustration notwithstanding, you ultimately accomplish your aim and that you have a good time doing it.

Becoming acquainted with local researchers immediately legitimises your research and presence in an area, and shows your willingness to be involved in local projects. You are, after all, more likely to gain permission to dig a series of pits in an area if you are affiliated to group of people already doing so. In working with a local group, the provision of transportation to out-of-the-way field sites may, in addition, open up a plethora of new investigative opportunities, allowing you and your equipment to go to places you never dreamed possible, though ultimately you are reliant on availability of, and access to, a vehicle and its driver. The independence of solitary fieldwork in such cases needs necessarily to be replaced by flexibility and an enforced lack of concern for time constraints.

By associating with people *au fait* with the area you intend to work in, it may be possible to receive insider feedback on the feasibility and practicality of *your* project from people "in the know", and so to make slight amendments (or wholesale changes) to your planned course of action. Involving yourself with local investigations, moreover, avoids the potential hostility that can sometimes be encountered by foreign fieldworkers who proceed along very insular lines of investigation, employing little or no local advice, and drafting in "experts" from their home country.

Working with a local group not only eliminates the insecurity prevalent with solitary fieldwork, but brings instant comradeship, moral support and, perhaps more pragmatically, a ready source of labour. Time spent digging pits, surveying vast tracts of land, fieldwalking, soil sampling, and coring lake beds can be reduced with several "field assistants", though methodological approaches may well be variable in such cases, leading to niggling concerns over consistency. Moreover, the old adage of "too many cooks" can all too soon become reality. While coring a lake bed in central Mexico, the on-board presence of several local university student assistants and the *omni*presence of their lecturer (equipped with camcorder and stylish directorial instruction, to record the events of the day), detracted from the matter in hand, and more significantly persistently undermined the stability and anchorage of the boat and hence, the accuracy with which the corer was lowered into the water and lake bed sediments. Similarly, one American professor, working in the same area, recently commented on the "veritable entourage" of spectators brought along to assist in a land surveying project, as a convoy of VW mini vans, piled high with local and exchange students, volcanologists, geologists, archaeologists, wives, mothers, cousins, dumpy levels and picnic panniers, pulled up at the arranged meeting place.

Working with local researchers is a mutual operation, and it should be remembered that involving other people in your work necessarily entails some input on your part into their investigations. This can prove to be demanding, given that while you may learn new sampling and analytical techniques, or be introduced to another area of interest, you will inevitably feel that a good part of the time you set aside for your fieldwork has been spent helping other people do theirs. It is more likely, however, that such activity will add value to the time you do spend on your own work, given that co-operation is likely to be much more forthcoming. Moreover, it is possible to glean an insight into what lines of investigation are considered to be important in the host country, and offers the potential to incorporate or compare their findings with those of your own.

TRAVELING ALONE WITH EQUIPMENT AND SAMPLES

Traveling light is desirable, but not always an option when undertaking foreign fieldwork, especially when you are reliant on public transport and do not have a "permanent" base in an area. As you struggle down the three flights of steps towards the coach stand, plastic bin liners full of wet sediment in hand, rucksack on your back (loaded with books, two tee shirts and a pair of plimsoles -you had to discard most of your clothing to make room), sombrero and stuffed donkey for Grandma strapped precariously to the back, occasionally clouting some passer by as you innocently turn round, there will undoubtedly be some heroic figure waiting to assist you in your quest. Be warned, however, that such chivalry is rarely free, or, for that matter, trustworthy. Be wary of anybody offering to help carry pieces of equipment or carefully acquired samples, given that the peculiar stimulates curiosity, and any commodity is potentially saleable. Regardless of their uselessness to any individual other than the researcher involved, for example, a set of sediment filled pipes obviously appealed to a youngster at Morelia bus station, who having offered to assist the overburdened student, darted off with the aforementioned pipes to his mates at the local liquor store, swiftly followed by his fraught victim and the burly, whistle-wielding luggage attendant. Having retrieved the said samples, not only did the youngster demand some recompense, but the hero of the day also hovered expectantly as the student in question queued for her bus ticket. It is perhaps worth having some change or home currency, much in demand "for the collection" to hand as a pay off in such situations, though in many cases it is best to follow your intuition and avoid any offers of assistance that might bring you, or your samples into a potentially hazardous situation.

GETTING YOUR SAMPLES HOME

As well as all the documentation associated with getting your samples home, there is the practical issue of how to do it, and the safest way of accomplishing this task successfully having got this far. Perhaps the most logical way to ensure the safe return of your samples is to carry them with you as hand luggage on your flight home. This ensures that you'll be there to answer any questions customs and airline officials might have, and reduces the probability of them getting lost. This may be practically impossible due to the bulk, size or weight of the samples and this necessarily needs to be borne in mind before departure. The amount of weight you can carry on a flight is strictly limited and exceeding your allowance will result in extra charges. Airlines will sometimes be very accommodating about carrying extra weight and can, in certain situations, waver charges, provided you explain your circumstances to them and do this well before the time of your departure. British Airways has done this for the both of us. Airlines tend to be less impressed by postgraduate students turning up with 300kg of samples on the day of the flight, and may impose hefty charges costing hundreds rather then tens of pounds. Carrying large, bulky or heavy pieces of equipment can bring the same response.

If the airline is reluctant to waver fees or reduce charges, you may have to return your samples by air or sea freight. Sending samples home by sea is considerably cheaper than air freight, though they may lie in dockside storage for months and can take a lot longer to reach their destination. The risk associated with returning samples unattended is much greater and we have heard nightmare stories of material being lost or contaminated both in storage and in transit. If you have collected enough of every sample, it may be useful to split and catalogue what you have prior to departure. Separating your samples and leaving them somewhere safe before you leave ensures that if anything gets lost in transit, that there is a back up batch to rely on, ensuring that all the efforts of your fieldwork are not lost. Cataloging your samples before departure ensures that any samples that are missing can be easily identified and can save on the number of samples that have to be retrieved from the back up batch should something go wrong.

Labeling your samples during sampling and for return home, is an important process and should be included in your fieldwork timetable. Several different methods of labeling should be used on the inside and outside of the sample container. It is not unusual, however, for sample labels to rub off or become detached during transit, even where indelible markers have been used. A combination of writing directly on the sample packaging and tagging external and internal to the sample (if possible) is recommended. Labeling the top and bottom of a sediment core or section upon retrieval may seem obvious, but can be crucial to any analysis you plan to undertake. There is nothing more frustrating than returning home and being unable to identify your samples correctly, because of insufficient labeling, because labels have been removed, or writing that was, is no more. If your samples can be contaminated or destroyed by being opened, by getting wet or moved around too much, it would be prudent to label your samples explaining what they are, or by including an official letter, preferably on headed notepaper, detailing the precautions necessary to be taken to avoid damage or contamination. What might seem excessive at the time might prove to be your salvation later.

When bringing samples out of a country it can ease things to have a letter from a home institution stating that the samples are of no commercial value; this can reduce a stay in customs from hours or days, to minutes. If possible, a copy of your letter in English and another in the language of your host country should be prepared for both overseas and home customs. A hastily written letter on headed notepaper, signed by "a lecturer" from the city university only hours before Georgina was due to fly home, for example, proved invaluable during a verbal wrangle in the customs office in Mexico City airport.

When bringing samples back into Britain it is important to consider what implications your terminology of the samples can have. The use of the term "soil" can result in a lengthy stay in quarantine given the regulations of the Ministry of Agriculture, and it may be better to employ terminology such as "geological specimens". Such are the many considerations that need to be taken into account when taking materials out of one country and bringing them into another.

CONCLUSIONS

We have dealt here with a series of what we believe to be aspects crucial to the work of a physical geographer in developing areas. Though we have hoped to consider some of the more important subject areas, we have mainly drawn on personal experience and those of people known to us, and we respect that individual fieldworkers will encounter very different circumstances and situations to the ones detailed above. Ultimately, each project is unique and the range of problems that the individual may encounter will inevitably vary from our own. Nevertheless, it is hoped that, in conjunction with the information provided elsewhere in this publication, the reader will be able to prepare themselves for what will hopefully lead to a successful research project and what will undoubtedly become remembered as one of the most exciting periods of their life.

4.

FROM TEACHER TO TAXI DRIVER: REFLECTIONS ON RESEARCH ROLES IN DEVELOPING AREAS

Elsbeth Robson

INTRODUCTION[1]

Conducting any social science research involving people inevitably engages the researcher in personal social relations with the researched, unless s/he relies exclusively on data collected by someone else. For postgraduates, direct data collection is usually deemed an essential part of the research project. Such research, whether based on interviews, observation, or other methodologies, involves social interaction which places the researcher in relations with the researched and sometimes also with research assistants.

This chapter is intended for a postgraduate audience and is written with those embarking on field research in developing areas in mind. In this chapter I explore the notion that a researcher adopts, or is forced into, certain roles when operating in the field. I am particularly concerned with those roles the researcher as 'outsider' may play and have no direct experience with which to consider the particular issues facing those who do research within their own social, or cultural, communities.[2] In the chapter I draw on my own recent experiences, as a British postgraduate student, of doing both quantitative and qualitative research in the rural

[1] Acknowledgements: I am grateful to the Economic & Social Research Council; Linacre College; School of Geography, Oxford University; the Beit Fund and the Dudley Stamp Memorial Fund which funded the research and fieldwork which stimulated this paper. The fieldwork would not have been possible without the assistance of Ibrahim Mohammed and Rakiya Baba Abubakar, and the co-operation of the citizens of Zarewa. I also thank Roberto Tibana and Katie Willis for their useful comments on earlier drafts of this paper, as well as Jill Robson for her meticulous proof reading.
[2] See Panini (1991) for a collection of essays by predominantly Asian women who carried out research in their home country, or among people of their own culture and language yet faced particular problems because of their personal background. Their gender, marital status, wealth, education, lifestyle etc. all affected the roles open to them during fieldwork. See also Uwem Ite's contribution to this monograph.

Hausa settlement of Zarewa in Kano State, Northern Nigeria.[3] This chapter reflects on the various roles researchers may choose, or may find thrust upon them, in the research environment. I hope that the reflective, rather than merely autobiographical, nature of the account I present here is useful. My aim is to help those embarking on fieldwork to think about fieldwork roles before they enter the research environment and to ask the questions 'What kind of role would be the most suitable for obtaining the information desired?' and 'What role is one likely to be given, or be expected to conform to?'[4]

In the first part of the chapter I examine some of the ascribed and manageable factors influencing a researcher's role in the field. The second part of the chapter looks at the difficulties in managing relationships with the researched and with research assistants. Finally, I conclude that the impact of the researcher in generating data must be recognised and the researcher's roles and relations in the field should be constantly monitored and modified in order to enhance the quality of the data being collected.

FINDING/BEING GIVEN FIELD ROLES

In some field situations the researcher may have no choice about the role(s) s/he is given, or has to adopt. It is logical for the members of a community being studied to attempt to explain and 'place' an outsider who appears as a stranger in their midst. Thus, it is not uncommon for myths about the researcher to arise within the research community. For example, (as researchers elsewhere have experienced) people in Zarewa at times thought I was a CIA agent!

The roles researchers are placed in are influenced by both 'ascribed' and 'manageable' factors about a researcher's identity. Ascribed factors can not be adapted to, so they have to be accepted. These include gender, religion, socio-economic positioning, age and ethnicity. There are also other factors which can be managed so a researcher usually has at least some choice about them e.g. living arrangements, the methodology used, how the researcher is introduced into the community, any intervention or involvement of the researcher in community activities and so on.

---

[3] My fieldwork study of a single village embraced a number of methodologies in a multiple strategy approach including formal questionnaire-based interviews, participant observation, informal interviews and time use observation.

[4] A useful discussion of field roles for the ethnographer, although it is not especially concerned with undertaking research in developing areas, is in Hammersley & Atkinson (1983) (especially chapter 4 on field relations).

Ascribed factors
Socio-economic positioning

It is almost always the case that postgraduates from richer countries researching in developing countries are wealthier, have more formal education and a more privileged socio-economic background than their research subjects.[5] Because of the iniquitous economic relations between the so-called 'developed' and 'developing' areas of the world, merely by locating to a new social environment in a 'developing' area researchers from 'developed' countries are shuffled in the social hierarchy, usually moving up the social scale. Being (or being perceived to be) positioned high up the socio-economic scale can be difficult for researchers - being 'rich' in Nigerian terms was something I had to cope with.[6]

One way I dealt with the problem of socio-economic positioning was by avoiding unnecessary displays of ostentatious wealth. While in the field I always stressed that I was a student on a small grant living without any financial assistance from my family. More specifically, for example, I concealed the fact that I had my own notebook computer and portable printer as research tools. In a situation where even university professors are dependent on unreliable secretaries, ancient typewriters, and poor stationery supplies I felt it politic not to flaunt my high-tech equipment. But, in fact, my 'superior' resources were totally useless when the electricity on campus was cut off for days - not a rare occurrence.

One indication of wealth, which became unavoidable for me, was the acquisition of a car. Originally I had been all in favour of the barefoot, low-tech approach, believing that researchers should arrive in villages on foot, by bicycle, or by local public transport and thus, avoid the problems of being a high profile VIP.[7] Although public transport was cheap (for me), so were the running costs of a car and depending on public transport to get to and from Zarewa village would have been extremely difficult and time consuming. Having a car also had other advantages. I was able to give lifts to villagers (space permitting) and on one occasion I was commissioned as a taxi driver to take one of the village chief's wives to visit bereaved kin in a neighbouring village. In this instance my efforts and the expense of overpriced illegally distributed petrol (the only fuel available) was more than repaid with hospitality, gifts of mangoes, two local cooking pots, and three baby pigeons!

---

[5] Mustapha (1993) refers to 'dollar-toting researchers' coming to Africa and particularly Nigeria in the 1990s.

[6] See also Nuala Bryce Gormley's contribution in this volume for further consideration of this issue.

[7] See Robert Chambers (1983) for the call of such a low-profile approach for the outside researcher, or development worker.

'While keen to offer lifts, Lisa never thought her Landrover would break a record for the number of passengers on four wheels'

Later I shall discuss the researcher as rich patron and describe further how I coped with the consequences of my high socio-economic status.

Gender, Age and Marital Status

The factors of gender and age, and perhaps to a lesser extent, marital status cannot be managed as part of the 'personal front' presented by the researcher in the field. They are important aspects of the identity of the researcher which affect the roles open to him/her, but also affect relationships with the researched and ultimately influence the type and quality of data collected.[8] Researchers may use (or try to avoid) common

---

[8] It has been recognised that the gender of the researcher and the researched affects the data produced. See, for example, Graham (1983) and Oakley (1981).

gender stereotypes to their advantage. Where women are culturally seen as unthreatening they may be able to obtain access and information more easily than a man.[9] It is equally the case that, where gender segregation is the norm, men may find entry to the world of women impossible and vice versa. Age differences, although they are also significant in determining field roles, <u>can</u> be overcome, for example, it is not impossible for adults to research the life worlds of children.

As a woman doing my research in a Hausa community I had great advantages over a man in the same situation because I had easy and unproblematic access to the domestic sphere and the world of women. Hausa society is strictly segregated by gender and, because of the religio-cultural seclusion of married women within their husband's house by the practice of purdah, adult men may not freely enter the homes of non-kin. However, as a woman I could enter any house unannounced and without prior arrangement. At the same time, I was sufficiently 'foreign' and 'different' from local women also to be able to relate to the world of men in some senses as an 'honorary man'.

Gender cannot be separated from the factor of marital status in determining my role in the field. As an unmarried woman I had the advantage of having a status akin to girls in Hausa society who, until they are married, have great mobility and are free to move about the streets and public places as well as to enter any house. However, my advanced age for a '*yarinya*' (girl) meant my status was completely anomalous - most of the girls in Zarewa are married by the age of 15, or earlier, and from then on restricted to their husband's house by the practice of wife seclusion. My non-conformity to the Hausa social constructions of female gender meant I was able to define my own spheres of movement. But the ambiguity of my status in Hausa terms meant there was always intense speculation in Zarewa about my marital status and it was a constant topic of conversation and enquiry. Being 'interrogated' in this way about one's personal life is not an uncommon experience for foreign researchers.[10]

---

[9] For a very interesting set of fieldwork accounts by women anthropologists in which the gender identity of the researcher is problematised, see Golde (1970). Sarah Howard also discusses this in her chapter.

[10] See for example Nigel Barley's (1983 & 1986) humorous accounts of his anthropological experiences in Cameroon where he suffered from the community's great curiosity about himself. In a similar vein reflecting on her twenty years of research involvement in India, Barbara Harriss-White (1993) speaks of being 'pelted with searching questions about my own life'.

Religion

Religion is another factor of a researcher's identity which, depending on the circumstances, may be irrelevant, or may be very important. It is not something which is necessarily as fixed as gender, age, or marital status and can, perhaps, sometimes be concealed. Before commencing fieldwork I thought a lot about the fact I was intending as a non-Muslim to do research in a Muslim community. I made an effort to learn about Islam and sought advice from others more knowledgeable about Northern Nigeria. I was warned against pretending to be a Muslim as a way of seeking greater acceptance. In fact it would have been impossible to have kept up any pretence. But being a non-Muslim living in a Muslim Hausa village had certain implications: I avoided performing ablution and prayer rituals five times a day, as well as fasting from dawn to dusk during Ramadan.[11] I was also able to be less strict than the village women about dress - although I took care always to dress modestly, I did not veil myself when out in public. Not being Muslim meant there was no opposition to my freedom of movement around the village and, unlike my Muslim research assistant Rakiya, I did not have to endure lectures on good Muslim behaviour for women.[12]

As far as religion was concerned, I was anxious not to be seen as a non-believer, or worse, an atheist. Therefore, I decided to make my membership of the Catholic Church a relevant aspect of my role in the field. So on the occasions I was asked '*Kin yi sallah?*' 'Do you pray?' meaning 'Are you a Muslim?'; I answered I was a Christian and that I went to church. Indeed I regularly attended Mass on Sundays when I was not in the village because the nearest Catholic church was in the university town where I spent my 'time off'. This meant to the villagers that my religious practices were essentially invisible or private, and perhaps therefore, I could not avoid the suspicion of being an 'immoral infidel'. My unmarried status and denial of having any marriage plans may also have contributed towards such an attitude, which surfaced occasionally, although I was keen to assure everyone otherwise. As a non-Muslim a kind of pity was also

---

[11] As it was I had no choice but to enter a partial fast during the month of Ramadan because it would have been very awkward to eat while everyone else was fasting and no food was prepared at midday anyway. However, I did drink water and suck boiled sweets, but only in view of my research assistants and in secret I ate biscuits. In this way I found the fasting period manageable.

[12] Other non-Muslim women who have done research in Muslim communities have reported similar advantages being a woman and having access to women, while at the same time being foreigners who could establish non-conventional roles in relation to men unlike any female members of the community. See, for example, Jeffrey (1979) and Papanek (1974).

sometimes expressed towards me by the villagers and jokes made about teaching me to perform the ritual Islamic prayers.

Ethnicity

Being white and European was part of my racial, or ethnic, identity as a foreigner in Nigeria and I can only speculate about the difference it would have made to my research roles if I were of different ethnicity. It is not simply a matter of skin colour - even if I were black and European I would have still been viewed as an outsider by Nigerians (in Hausaland black Europeans and North Americans find themselves addressed as '*Bature*' or '*Baturiya*', terms meaning European man, or woman but which are used to refer to all westerners regardless of their colour). If I were Hausa, clearly my position would have been one of an insider, but doubtless still removed from the villagers in terms of wealth and educational status. Speaking fluent Hausa would have been an advantage and being thereby (in all likelihood) Muslim would possibly have been of benefit in terms of closer rapport and better cultural understanding. But there remain elements of outsider status even for Hausa women who undertake fieldwork in Hausaland, due to urban, wealth and education status.[13]

Manageable Factors
Living Arrangements

Where the researcher is resident in the community, living arrangements are an important matter which can seriously affect the success, or otherwise, of the research. Sometimes the researcher will have little or no choice about where to stay.[14] On my first preliminary visit to Zarewa village I stayed with the village chief's eldest son, his wife and their three young sons, but it rapidly became clear to me that it would not be a suitable arrangement for long term residence if I was to complete successful fieldwork. Firstly, the wife of the household was clearly burdened by 'looking after' me and generally treating me like an important guest. Although I reckoned that with time I could become a more accepted member of the household, I also knew I could never be fully integrated because of my anomalous status as a single, unmarried woman. Neither

---

[13] See Imam, 1993, pp. 233-235 for example. See also Uwem Ite's chapter in this volume about outsider status 'at home'.

[14] Jane Carter (1991), for example, doing research on ethnoforestry in the Himalayas recalls how she arrived for the first time in the Nepali village where she was to do fieldwork. To reach the village she had trekked a long distance alone and was so tired that she was unable to do any more than be welcomed to the village head's house, be fed and put to bed. She remained resident in his household throughout her stay and had no choice in the matter.

was I prepared to jeopardise my research by spending time sharing the burden of household chores which integration as a participant female member of daily household life would entail - if anyone would even let me do housework.[15] I also thought I could possibly be perceived as a threat to the couple's marital relationship being young, female and single. In addition, there was no room in the house I could conveniently make my own. Even if there had been, I doubted that I could have retained my sanity trying to write fieldnotes in the close confines of the small residential compound which was constantly filled with children and visitors who regarded me as a kind of entertaining spectacle - an object of much curiosity and endless fascination which they came to touch, laugh and stare at.

A solution was reached whereby my research assistants and I decided to occupy an empty house belonging to another of the village chief's sons who had successfully migrated to Kano, the state capital city. Like typical Hausa compounds the house consisted of rooms around a courtyard, but unusually had two entrances. This proved to be a good fieldwork base because it provided peace and quiet in which to write up fieldnotes and recuperate from the rigours of the heat and the stresses of interviewing. However, not living in a family household meant some loss in opportunity for close participant observation of household relations.[16] Living at times alone in the house, but more often together with my two research assistants, sometimes caused raised eyebrows (mostly about who slept where), but thankfully there were enough rooms for moral and personal sensibilities to be respected. At various times we had to share the house with others, including a Koranic teacher and his assortment of young male students who were rendered shelterless when one night in the rainy season the mud roof of their hut collapsed. During another period we had to share the house with one of the village chief's unmarried sons who occupied a room when he was in the village for weekends or on leave from his government job in Kano. Some rooms in 'our' house were also used for storage of grain and fertiliser.

MULTIPLE ROLES

In this section I discuss the multiple and often dichotomous roles I found myself playing during fieldwork. I was a woman but also an 'honorary' man in some situations, an insider and an outsider, a friend and a stranger, a teacher and a learner, a giver and a taker. Often it was difficult to juggle

---

[15] See Clare Madge's contribution to this volume for further discussion of this point.
[16] Some researchers may decide, like Elizabeth Francis (1992), that living with a family is worth the sacrifice of privacy for what is gained in terms of respectability, a sense of belonging and information derived from close contact with household members.

these various roles simultaneously. I explore here in more detail the implications of some of the roles I played, or was expected to play, as rich patron, teacher and friend.

Researcher as Rich Patron

Being perceived as rich is an unavoidable part of being European in Nigeria. Expectations were high about my wealth and generosity as I was following a long stream of expatriate researchers from Europe and America. Many people in the village (and the university) were eager that on my final departure to England I should 'dash' them my belongings. People frequently asked to be given my car, radio, kettle, mosquito net, camera etc. believing I would no longer need them and/or could simply buy new ones. Promises were often made about buying these things from me, but the Nigerian economic crisis meant that such amounts of cash were beyond the resources even of university lecturers. I was not often directly asked for money except by those who considered themselves in patron-client relations with me. My research assistants, Rakiya and Ibrahim, both asked me for money on a couple of occasions and I responded with gifts, or wage advances. At the Muslim festivals of Eid, and on my departure, I gave both of them gifts in cash and kind. I also invited them to my house for celebratory occasions like my birthday and treated them with hospitality whenever they came to call on me in my university accommodation.

Despite these efforts, I often wondered if I did too little for my assistants, or too much. I found it hard to know where the line lay between a just and an exploitative relationship. Wasn't the whole enterprise of me being in Nigeria as a foreign research student externally funded in hard currency by the former colonial power, while Nigerian research institutions crumbled in economic collapse, intrinsically exploitative? Trying to treat my research assistants fairly may have been somewhat insignificant in the light of the injustice of the global set up.

Having a camera and taking photographs as part of my research also became a problematic aspect of being in the role of rich patron. I wanted to take photographs illustrating different aspects of the local economy and social organisation to use in my thesis and for teaching. Using my camera as a research tool led to frequent requests for photographs. These requests were difficult to contain within limits of what I could afford and handle. There was an insatiable demand from the villagers for photographs of themselves which I could never meet, even if they were prepared to pay for the photographs (as they sometimes said they were). However, I felt it was inappropriate to ask them for payment. After each long fieldwork period in 1992 and 1993 I sent/gave large numbers of prints to those villagers portrayed in the pictures I took. But I am sure they felt cheated because I could not provide a copy of every snapshot I ever took, nor could I give one copy to each person in every picture.

In general, taking photographs caused a lot of difficulties and was a very uncomfortable part of the fieldwork. Villagers became demanding that I should come and take their picture and if I did then every time they saw me after that would insistently want to know where their picture was. That led me to only taking my camera out on special occasions and carrying it concealed in a bag so people would not see it and demand to have their picture taken. It was also frustrating because I wanted to be able to take natural pictures. However, the villagers had very set ideas about photography and unless they were unaware they were being photographed, would insist on putting on their best clothes and pose rigidly for the camera with very serious expressions, women always with downcast eyes. Our differing expectations about me and my camera were difficult to reconcile amicably and on occasions there were near fights over who should pose in front of my lens and who should get to keep the pictures I brought! Overall, despite the difficulties involved in taking pictures, I feel it was worthwhile because they are a valuable record and I was able to give at least something back by providing some people with some photographs.

Researcher as teacher
During my fieldwork in Zarewa I often found myself in the role of informal teacher. Not only as teacher to my research assistants, who although they were university undergraduates had never heard of Hitler or understood the meaning of apartheid, but also to the villagers themselves. We had impromptu discussions of many things from apartheid to homosexuality - often prompted by listening to the BBC World Service on my battery powered short wave radio. Their thirst for knowledge and capability for incredulity never ceased to surprise me. There was amazement when I talked about homelessness and poverty in Britain and reluctant disbelief when I described beggars on London streets. Thus we learnt much from each other.

Being highly educated (in western terms) also placed me in the role of teacher. Once or twice during the fieldwork when visiting women in their homes for interviews, they would ask me to teach them. One woman was very insistent that I should teach her, although she was unclear about what it was she wanted to learn. Another woman, a young wife without any children, asked me to teach her to read and write and so did the wife and mother in our 'adopted' family. Although I would have liked to be able to teach them literacy skills and personally felt very disturbed about the massive gender inequalities in education which served to keep women illiterate, I felt I could not oblige because it was not for that purpose I came to Zarewa village. I hadn't the time, nor other resources, at my disposal. I reasoned 'How could I teach one or two women and not all the others I knew?', and 'What would happen when I left - who would continue the work?'. Perhaps I could have found a way to involve the village in literacy programmes, but I retained my stance that it was not my role to intervene in a way that could directly challenge the status quo. I don't know if I did the right thing.

Although I resisted becoming a formal teacher, the women and men I came into contact with in Zarewa perhaps learned some things from me - maybe little in comparison with what I learned from them. During interviews we made opportunities for interviewees to ask any question they wished. Men in particular asked with interest about life in England. Frequent questions were about food, farming, weather, climate, and marriage - all important themes in Hausa life. Naturally, some people were more interested than others to know what life was like in '*Ingila*' and where I came from.

Researcher as friend

One of the difficulties in maintaining the best role for the effectiveness of my research developed after I had been in the field for some time. It became clear that many of the villagers, and in particular women, liked me to visit them in their homes. They wanted me to come often and to talk, but they did not want to be interviewed nor answer the questions I wanted to pose. At first they co-operated with my requests for information out of goodwill, politeness and perhaps a sense of duty. Later many of them wanted to see me only as a friend. I was eager to maintain friendly relationships with all the villagers and indeed was very upset on the rare occasion when we inadvertently offended someone. Unfortunately my fluency in Hausa was insufficient for me to be involved in common daily conversation on an equal level and ask the questions I wanted without using Rakiya, or Ibrahim, as my interpreter. It was difficult and interview schedules were unfinished because people refused to co-operate any further, although they still welcomed our visits and were happy to sit and exchange daily chit-chat. I found this very frustrating and realise that only a very long investment of time spent improving my Hausa and perhaps working with a different female assistant could change this situation. We were partly to blame for the fact that women began to resent us coming to ask questions perhaps because we overloaded them with too many interview visits. But even in situations where participant observation is used as the sole method of ethnographic research, the researcher has to be careful that s/he remains critical and distanced from relations with the researched so as not to slip into the trap of comfortable friendship.

I was especially careful not to become over friendly with my research assistants, keeping some distance was necessary for the maintenance of our good working relations.

Researcher as unfortunate marginal

It is common for the researcher on entering the research environment to find him/herself in the role of naive idiot. This may be helpful at first because it allows the researcher to learn about things like a child.[17] This is a role which changes with time as the researcher becomes more familiar with the unknown culture and able to adapt. Although my ability to converse in Hausa improved throughout the time I was in the field, I was pitied because of my lack of fluency and inability to perform many daily tasks done by women, such as cooking and pounding food with a large heavy wooden pestle and mortar. Generally, the first time a Hausa person saw me wearing Hausa dress, eating local food, plaiting a girl's hair, picking up a crying child, pulling water from the well or speaking in Hausa they were astounded, amazed and flattered. To my pleasure I was sometimes complimented and told '*Kina 'yar Zarewa*' (You are a daughter of Zarewa).

My personal characteristics also positioned me in the role of unfortunate marginal. People felt sorry for me because I was 'still' unmarried in my mid-twenties. In Hausa terms this gave me the status of a girl and a child. In this respect I was regarded as an oddity for whom the villagers felt pity because I had obviously been unsuccessful in getting a husband - they said surely I was missing out on happiness. Villagers also expressed pity for me because they knew I was in a foreign land away from my home and family.

CHANGES IN ROLES OVER TIME

One hopes that over time in the field the researcher's role will change - hopefully in the direction of greater adaptation and acceptance.[18] Particularly in the early days, I occupied the role of 'incompetent' student learning about Nigerian and Hausa ways of life to which I gradually

---

[17] The anthropologist Marjorie Shostak describes the awkward and embarrassing experiences of trying to adjust to Kalahari life. She says at first "... I pointed, pantomimed, and repeatedly asked my two questions: 'What is the name for that?' and 'When I do this, what is it called?' "(1990, 17-18).

[18] Marjorie Shostak (op. cit.) recounts how, as a visiting anthropologist, she was slowly accepted by the !Kung hunter gatherers in Botswana and eventually felt able to count some of them as her friends.

adapted. Later on I came to realise that I was not always as ignorant as I thought because my in-depth reading of the ethnographic literature of Hausaland meant I was as well, if not sometimes better, informed about some things than Rakiya and Ibrahim. Although they were Muslim and Hausa by birth, both had grown up on a university campus and in urban suburbs respectively. They too had their eyes opened by participating in and researching village life with me.

The following incident is an example of how I and my research assistants adapted our roles in the village over time. Throughout the first long period of fieldwork in 1992 Rakiya, Ibrahim and I occupied the *shago* of 'our' house in Zarewa village. We more or less lived in this one room which had only one window and a door which opened directly to the path outside. Many of our daily activities were performed just outside our door in what was essentially public space and people were continually walking past the open door of the room. Children frequently teased us by banging on the metal door, calling out and coming to sit and stare. Ibrahim slept in another room inside the house, but during our 1992 fieldwork period the inside of the house was essentially abandoned and unused. For example, we could not use the polluted well in the house and always took our baths at the neighbouring compound of our 'adopted family'.

Later on, during the second phase of research in 1993, I became increasingly uncomfortable with these arrangements and decided we should move inside the house to occupy a more private space where we would not have to sit in the street for coolness in the evenings, nor would we have to carry out our daily living in more, or less, public view. I had also become more aware of how our living arrangements contravened Hausa norms - a *shago* is a man's own room and it is only men who sit around outside on the street. Women keep inside the houses almost all the time. So Rakiya and I moved inside the house and Ibrahim occupied the *shago*, thus reflecting the usual Hausa gender divisions of domestic space. Furthermore, our living in one room in a rough and ready kind of way made us akin to Koranic students who are essentially beggars with low status. Thus as I settled into my fieldwork role I gradually adopted a more locally appropriate set of living arrangements.

During fieldwork in 1992 my father came to visit me in Nigeria and in 1993 my mother, 'stepfather' and sister also came. During both trips we went to visit Zarewa for a day. Throughout the fieldwork I carefully resisted taking any of my colleagues from the nearby university to the village because I wanted to avoid 'rural tourism', but I was very keen that my relatives should meet some of the villagers. The reasons were that not only did I know it would be an eye-opening and interesting experience for my family to visit the village, but perhaps more importantly because I wanted the villagers to know me in a more concrete way. I knew that for them to meet some of my relatives would be significant in enabling them to place me in a more solid context. Who you are in Hausa society is to an extent partly determined by who you are related to. I also knew that bringing my family to Zarewa all the way from *'Ingila'*, as it were, was a statement about how important the people of Zarewa were to me. On both occasions the villagers were delighted to meet my family and it improved the level of my acceptance and rapport.

In this section I have focused on multiple roles, but roles in the field are not static - they change over time. They need a lot of effort, careful awareness and monitoring on the part of the fieldworker to be beneficially maintained over the period of the field research and even after the researcher returns 'home'.

RESEARCH RELATIONS
Relations with the Researched

Relations between the researcher and the researched are rarely, if ever, equal. It is critical that we remain conscious of the socio-economic and other inequalities which exist between 'researchers' and 'researched', as well as between 'insiders' and 'outsiders'. The relations between researcher and researched leave neither unchanged. It would be naive to think that the approach of 'take nothing but photographs and leave nothing but footprints' is applicable to research involving people and human communities. Even for research on physical environments that may be nothing more than a utopian dream. I am not going to speculate here in detail about the impact of my research on the village community in Zarewa. All I can say is that my presence in the village, and now my absence, cannot be without consequences. At the community level I am thankful that there do not appear to be any expectations that I could act as an advocate to government, or other, institutions to bring the village development and progress - or whatever. This is probably for several reasons. Firstly, the village community is well connected to the local and state governments through its own (male) élite. It is one of the larger settlements in the local government area, so Zarewa has managed to get its own share of the national cake with the establishment within the last decade of a borehole, bank, secondary school, health centre and electricity supply. Furthermore, it was well understood that I was a research student, from the university, without any links to development NGOs or other institutions.[19] In fact, from early on in the research I was treated in a very informal and joking

---

[19] Elsewhere in this volume Simon Batterbury discusses the pros and cons of different institutional affiliations.

way by the village chief who obviously thought my work was of no serious consequence - this was no doubt linked to my age and gender status. Although it was something of an advantage to be left alone and I was able to get on with my work relatively unhindered, without demands being made of me, I could have benefited from serious discussions with the chief and his assistants among the elder men of the community.

After I left Nigeria one of the villagers wrote to me in a letter, "Your departure for home has been a serious problem because people have been asking where is Baturiya?[20] My answer always is you left for home and you will be back soon" (Letter from AKM 10/10/93). This letter also raises the issue of expectations. Having been in Zarewa on three research trips from 1991 to 1993 there is an expectation among the villagers that the personal relationships I forged there are important so it is natural I would go back again to visit people. However, much as I tried to explain to the villagers that my work in the village had come to an end and I did not know what my future plans might be, there was always plenty of good-natured banter about my coming back bringing my future husband and children to meet them, or better still, I would invite them to England for my wedding. Deep probing and intense questioning of my marital status and future marriage plans were something I experienced throughout my stay in the field. Despite not very serious offers, I made it clear that I did not intend to marry any of the village men - I said my mother would be unhappy at the idea because she would not see me if I married and lived in my husband's home so far away. Different researchers have dealt with related forms of this issue in different ways. Some 'invent' spouses, or partners, others do literally marry their subject - the stories are many and various. What is relevant to remember is that marital status (whether actual or perceived) is an important factor in determining the nature of relations with the researched and consequently the data collected.

It is often the case that the researcher benefits more in personal terms from the research (e.g. by gaining a higher degree) than the individuals who provide the research data. Especially at the level of

---

[20] In Hausa *Baturiya* means European woman and although I adopted a Hausa (but not a Muslim) name while in the field I was widely known in the village simply as *Baturiya*. I often felt very infuriated when children in particular, constantly called out '*Baturiya! Baturiya!*' at the sight of me so that an echoing chorus followed me whenever I moved around the village. I also found this a very depersonalising experience and felt that the use of *Baturiya* to address me meant I was labelled simply as a western woman thus, emphasising my whiteness, my otherness, but not recognising me as an individual person who had a name of her own. Sometimes I was confused for another white woman researcher working in a nearby town and markets. Although we are of similar height and build it is still a salutary reminder that even during a long term stay, the outside researcher still remains one of 'them'.

postgraduate research direct policy, or other useful applications of research are uncommon. Sooner, or later, the issues of reciprocity and debt to informants come to the fore and are agonised over by most researchers. It is nearly always the case that the researcher feels greatly indebted to the people who have provided much of their time and information which will be of direct benefit to the researcher in terms of career advancement. How to deal with this indebtedness is not a simple issue.[21] It can involve painful adjustments for thinking, caring researchers who want to be responsible and act ethically. One potential solution is for the researcher to take on the role of advocate on behalf of the researched in order to represent their interests to government, NGOs or other institutions. I do not discuss this possibility here because I have no direct experience of advocacy in research, however, Simon Batterbury's chapter in this volume does discuss some of the possibilities of mutually-beneficial affiliations. In the end, perhaps, the researcher has to accept that the debt to the researched can not be repaid.

During my research, I responded to the problem of reciprocity in various ways. When I was leaving the field I prepared a short report in English and Hausa about the village and its environs which included copies of the maps I had made of the village and its location. This was in response to requests made to me by the village school teachers for a booklet that they could use with primary school children. I gave copies to the primary school head teacher, the head teacher of the secondary school, the village head, the local government chairman (who lived in the village) and both my research assistants. It was very well received even by those with little, or no, literacy skills. Early on in the research I gave copies of the village sketch map I had drawn to nearly anyone who asked for it. It was much appreciated and enjoyed even by those who could not read, but who, with some explanations, could understand what was represented on the paper.

I also made a great effort after leaving the field to make copies of photographs I had taken of villagers and send them copies, as I have already mentioned above. This was much appreciated, but costly for me. When leaving the village I gave some of the household utensils to women who had been closest and most helpful during my stays in the village.

---

[21] Elizabeth Francis (1992) recounts how, during her research in a Luo community in Kenya, the problem of indebtedness to research informants became overwhelming. Although she was able to offer some token reciprocation by hosting large social gatherings at which refreshments were served and each guest went home with a small gift, she felt she could neither properly repay them for their assistance in her research, nor could she offer the help to find jobs and scholarships which was part of the expectations of her as an educated, urban outsider.

Furthermore, I continue to maintain albeit infrequent contact by letter with my research assistants and certain literate men of the village community.

The issue of paying, or reimbursing, informants (even in a token way) is a thorny problem for many researchers especially where there is a strong 'rich-poor' differential between the researcher and the researched and/or there has been a pattern of payment by previous researchers in the area.[22] I did not want to pay my research informants because of reluctance to set a precedent, or to create expectations that I might later find impossible to fulfil or which might create problems for future researchers. Besides, I did not have the financial resources at my disposal to pay everyone who talked to me, or agreed to be interviewed. Yet, after a while, it became clear that people rarely refused to talk and they were also very generous to me and my assistants. Women frequently gave myself and Rakiya food when we visited their compounds. I soon realised that I could not avoid being involved in gift exchange relations and if I consistently refrained from giving any gifts, or money, I would be seen as ungenerous and it could spoil our acceptance and good relations. So I began to make small gifts of soap, or biscuits bought from one of the village traders. I also reciprocated in other small ways. Whenever a woman we visited had something for sale like cooked food or snacks I insisted on buying some, even if she also wanted to give us some as a gift. When moving about the village I kept handfuls of sweets in my pockets to give to children - especially those who were scared and burst into tears at the sight of me. On the occasion of a birth, naming ceremony, sickness, wedding or death in any of the households with which we were acquainted I usually gave a small gift.

In participating in gift-exchange relations with women I tried to strike a balance between being sufficiently generous, yet not appearing to have money to throw away. On my final departure from the village we spent a day going around to visit each household where we had

---

[22] The issues of paying for information and interfering with the local economy were difficult dilemmas for Marjorie Shostak (1990) and her husband during anthropological research in Botswana. The !Kung demanded money, tobacco and jobs, but initially the anthropologists did not want to yield to pressure. They were reluctant to encourage moves from traditional ways of life, as well as being worried about the consequences in an economy where money had only recently been introduced and where their own presence was only short term. They grappled with the question of whether they should practise strict non-interference in local ways of life. Finally, they did pay for interviews with gifts, or money, partly because they followed a line of anthropologists who had handed out tobacco, paid informants and provided their vehicles to be used for food collecting trips. Eventually Marjorie and her husband had to accept relationships with the !Kung on their terms as well as accepting long term responsibility to work with them in the struggles to determine their own futures in time of great change.

interviewed or knew family members. On that occasion we said our good-byes and thanks, wished them well and gave a gift of sweets and biscuits. Likewise, at festivals I gave gifts of foodstuffs to the two or three households I knew most closely and had most involvement with. In fact, every time I visited the village I brought gifts of fruit (or on special occasions more expensive potatoes) from the city for the wife in our 'adopted' household and she shared them with her children, husband (if he was around) and neighbours (if enough) and any visitor who might be in the house at the time. In Hausa culture, gift giving and receiving is an important part of social relationships and the virtue of generosity is highly valued. I had to find a way of fitting into those cultural norms without compromising myself to meet demands which would be highly inappropriate, or making promises I would not be able to meet. I do not know how well I succeeded and it is an issue which on occasions made me intensely uncomfortable. On reflection, I realise that to pay people for interviews and help would have been highly inappropriate by converting a cultural practice of gift exchange into a commercial transaction.

I did not get it right much (any?) of the time. In the very early days of my research, before I had properly thought things through, when I tried to pay my first research helper, Salamatu, who was the 12 year old daughter of the junior secondary school principal, her father called me to ask why I was giving her so much money. Eventually he allowed her to keep the money, but I did not dare to pay her again in cash and risk his displeasure again. Instead I compromised with the gift of some exercise books and things for her schoolwork. We actually only worked together for a few days during my first preliminary research visit because it soon became clear that Salamatu's English and literacy skills were insufficient and she was too young to help me conduct serious interviews with adult women.

I did take gifts to people during one particularly arduous and difficult round of interviews concerned with household budgets which required each adult member of the selected household to recall itemised income and expenditure on a comprehensive lists of goods and services. Sometime into this round of interviews, as the going got sticky, we resorted to taking gifts of sweets, kola nut and biscuits to men and women in order to smooth the path of the interviews.

There can also be dangers of being too zealous and 'correct' about relations with informants which I hope the following example from my fieldwork may illustrate. In preparing the questionnaire for the round of household budget interviews I also prepared an introduction to precede each interview which explained the purposes of the research, the type of information we wanted to know, reassured informants that answers would be confidential, stressed that they had the right to refuse to answer any question if they wished and we would not be offended if they said a particular question was not a good one etc. This little speech was translated into Hausa and learnt by my assistants. However, we soon found that informants were disinterested and the whole speech required too long an attention span. So after the first couple of interviews we dropped the introductory recital because it was clearly inappropriate - normal Hausa conversation requires interactive conversation rather than soliloquies. I think this illustrates that researchers must be flexible and adapt their approach to field roles and relations without being too dogmatic. On reflection, in this particular instance it would have been better to give explanations and assurances as the interview progressed, as and when respondents were puzzled or inquisitive. To an extent that is what we did, because once Rakiya and Ibrahim had learnt the explanations and assurances they could express them as and when appropriate to try and ensure the smooth progress of the interview.

Research relations inevitably mean getting involved in people's lives. As researchers we are also thinking, feeling, human beings so that remaining totally objective and impersonal towards our research subjects is impossible. If researching people in situations of poverty or suffering, say AIDS sufferers in Uganda, refugees in Somalia, or shanty dwellers in São Paulo, it would be difficult not to be moved by their plight. Even archaeologists acknowledge that research can be emotionally traumatic even when the subjects are dead.[23] For many researchers, however, the lives of those they research can become a profound motivation to continue their work.

During fieldwork I became, to some extent, unavoidably personally and emotionally involved in the lives of the Zarewa villagers. Remaining, at least partially, as an observer, with the necessary distance which that requires, can be difficult at times. Yet we are instructed that over-rapport, or going 'native' and becoming a total participant, is not what is required for good research. My personal beliefs meant that generally I found it difficult to accept the social norms which governed the lives of women in Zarewa, denying them literacy unlike their brothers, marrying them early to older men and constraining them by purdah. Sometimes I became angry at the attitudes of men towards women and found myself biting my tongue to keep quiet. I was particularly disturbed by the number of maternal deaths in childbirth which happened while I was working in the village. Two

---

[23] Margaret Cox working on the social history of the eighteenth century London Huguenot community, through information provided by the corpses in the vaults of a Spitalfields church, found herself very distressed as she studied the causes of their deaths (Guardian 24/12/93).

other deaths were especially distressing for me. The first was a sickly baby girl of a very young mother. I had been given the child to hold and could see she was dying with terrible dehydration from diarrhoea. I believe the women in the family knew too that she was dying but were powerless through patriarchal gender relations and ignorance to seek treatment. The second distressing death was that of the oldest daughter of the school principal who eventually died of a long illness after many efforts at hospital treatment. Both families were well known to myself and my research assistants and we shared in their grief. Conversely, we also shared joyful occasions like the naming ceremony when a close friend and neighbour safely gave birth to her fourth son having lost one child in infancy and following a miscarriage the previous year.

Whether or not you are confronted with poverty or death, relations with the researched are essentially stressful as the researcher has to maintain and manage his/her position as a 'marginal native'. The feelings of 'schizophrenia', or betrayal, in resisting overidentification with the researched are inevitable: the temptation to conform in order to feel more comfortable should be resisted in order not to jeopardise objectiveness and critical faculties.[24]

Relations with research assistants

The relations between a researcher and research assistants are rarely, if at all, discussed in the literature. Yet, even Ph.D. students with relatively meagre research budgets are able to, and often do, employ research assistants when working in poorer countries. In many cases, fieldwork could not be carried out without the assistance of locals with insider knowledge. More than anything else assistants are employed for their language skills. Traditionally, anthropology has been the social science discipline which has stressed the importance of language learning for field research. More often the researcher's lack of fluency in a local language, or languages, forces her/him to depend on someone else who may not be that fluent in the researcher's own tongue. It is ironic, but sadly true that there are even eminent scholars who have never bothered to learn the language of the communities around which they have built their careers. Ideally, geographers would take the lead from anthropologists and place greater emphasis on the importance of language learning to carry out successful research. But language learning requires a large investment of time and effort which is rarely compatible with the pressure on students to complete the Ph.D. thesis within three years.

---

[24] Hammersley and Atkinson (1983).

While research assistants can help to collect more data in terms of quantity, the quality and reliability of the data need to be considered. It goes without saying that relations to research assistants should be professionally and ethically conducted in the same way as other relations with the researched, and with colleagues in the host, or academic, community. A common dilemma researchers face is the question of 'What is a fair wage to pay research assistants?'. When converted to the researcher's home, or hard currency, local wage rates may seem pitifully small, or equally likely, they may be beyond the capability of a postgraduate on a student research grant. If thinking of, or forced to, employ research assistants it is a good idea to ask around before agreeing wage levels. You also have to decide how to pay - daily, weekly, monthly, or per interview etc. Clearly, the skills and educational level of the research assistants should be taken into account. International institutions may set wage standards at a level above local standards. In Nigeria well-meaning colleagues cautioned me not to pay my assistants too much, or be too generous, towards them because it was said they would only take advantage - I was advised that it would not be good to be seen as a rich white outsider with pockets full of hard currency! Ultimately, it is the researcher's own choice. As well as wage levels, other aspects of employing research assistants including training, perks, benefits and person management need to be considered.

I employed two assistants, a man and a woman, who were undergraduate students in the university to which I was affiliated as a research associate for the duration of the fieldwork period. Both of the students were grateful for the money and the experience and would otherwise have been idle during the prolonged closure of Nigerian universities in 1992 and 1993 due to strikes and other disturbances. Handling the relationships with research assistants was for me one of the most difficult aspects of the fieldwork. The problem lay in our similarities and differences and the need for close teamwork. We were close in age, and were all unmarried, yet our cultural backgrounds were very different. Although we were all university students (albeit on two different continents) the gulfs between our educational and life experiences were immense. I found myself in the role of teacher and employer with people whom 'at home' I would normally share equal status.

There were also difficulties due to the nature of the fieldwork which made it necessary for the three of us to spend long periods in Zarewa living in very close proximity in a village which was 'home' to none of us. The stress of living in what was essentially a couple of rooms became unbearable at times and resulted in at least one major row during which Ibrahim quit. He later resumed our working relationship - partly because he needed the money, and also because I had agreed that I would write him references and letters of introduction when we completed the period of fieldwork. It was very hard for me to maintain a friendly, easy, relaxed relationship so that we could get on together sharing car journeys, eating together and sleeping under the same roof while simultaneously also retaining some kind of professional distance as an employer. It was a difficult position - in my 'normal' life as a Ph.D. student I play the roles of a student, a learner and a 'subordinate', but in the field roles were reversed and I found it difficult to be the teacher, the one deciding what we should do each day and directing my assistants to do work for me. The only previous experience I had like that was teaching children, but my assistants in Nigeria were adults, albeit young adults, and very close to me in age and generation. Yet I had very different positionality in terms of my skills and resources and that put me in a position of power.

With my research assistants I found it hard to maintain a balance between close friendliness and more distant 'professionalism'. Ideally I would have liked to have had co-researchers with whom to share decision making along the way about the direction and progress of the research. But in reality it was my research for my Ph.D., funded by my research award from the British government through the ESRC and I was employing Rakiya and Ibrahim to help me achieve my aims. Actually I could never have completed the research without them, unless I had spent considerably longer in the field and invested many more months in intensive language learning - an impossibility within the time frame imposed by my university and funding agency. The close relations my research assistants and I of necessity evolved were, however, not without their rewards and inspired a sincere support demonstrated in this extract from a letter from Ibrahim

> "...I am ready to ... do your any work ... and I am ready at any time, I would never relax or fail you until you succeed through your PH.D. I am wishing you success and the best always, and I am praying I should see your thesis" (Ibrahim Moh'd B.K. letter of 10.10.93)

CONCLUSIONS
In this chapter I have shown that finding an appropriate role for fieldwork is essentially a methodological problem. The researcher can have many different and often conflicting roles - friend, fellow student, patron, teacher and even taxi driver. Successful fieldwork involves learning how to handle the constraints and opportunities offered by the researcher's role(s) in the field. Some factors affecting roles can be anticipated and managed by the

researcher. Other factors simply have to be adapted to, like the gender, age and ethnicity of the researcher.

It has not been possible to discuss in detail here the links between the methods used in fieldwork and the resulting roles of the researcher. For example, anthropological-style in-depth immersion of the full-time participant observer requires a closer involvement with the researched than formal interviews. Recognising that the presence and role of the researcher has a significant impact on data generation this chapter has stressed that the researcher's roles and relations in the field should be constantly monitored and modified to enhance the quality of the data collected.

REFERENCES

Barley, Nigel 1983 The Innocent Anthropologist Harmondsworth: Penguin.

Barley, Nigel 1986 A Plague of Caterpillars Harmondsworth: Penguin.

Carter, Jane 1991 'Approaches to Development Studies' research seminar in Queen Elizabeth House, International Development Centre, University of Oxford, 1/3/91.

Chambers, Robert 1983 Rural Development: Putting the Last First Harlow: Longman.

Francis, Elizabeth 1992 'Qualitative research: Collecting life histories' in Stephen Deveraux & John Hoddinott (eds) Fieldwork in Developing Countries London: Harvester Wheatsheaf, 86-101.

Golde, Peggy (ed) 1970 Women in the Field: Anthropological Experiences Chicago: Aldine.

Graham, Hilary 1983 "Do her answers fit his questions?' Women and the survey method' in Eva Gamarnikow et al. (eds) The Public and the Private London: Heinemann.

Hammersley, Martyn & Atkinson, Paul (eds) 1983 Ethnography: Principles in Practice London: Routledge.

Harriss-White, Barbara 1993 'Research as disruption' Oxford Magazine 94 Wk2 TT, 7-10.

Imam, Ayesha Mei-Tje 1993 'If you won't do these things for me, I won't do seclusion for you: Local and regional constructions of seclusion ideologies and practices in Kano, Northern Nigeria.' Unpublished Ph.D. Thesis, University of Sussex.

Jeffrey, Patricia 1979 Frogs in a Well: Indian Women in Purdah London: Zed Press.

Mustapha, Abdul Raufu 1993 'Society and the social sciences in Northern Nigeria: 1962-1993' Paper presented to the African Studies Association Conference, Boston, Dec. 1993.

Oakley, Ann 1981 'Interviewing women: A contradiction in terms' in Helen Roberts (ed) Doing Feminist Research London: Routledge.

Panini, M. N. (ed) 1991 From the Female Eye: Accounts of Women Fieldworkers Studying Their Own Communities Delhi: Hindustan Publishing Corporation.

Papanek, Hannah J. 1974 'The woman fieldworker in a purdah society' Human Organization 23, 160-3.

Shostak, Marjorie 1990 (1st pub 1981) Nisa: The Life and Words of a !Kung Woman London: Earthscan.

5.

HOME, ABROAD, HOME: THE CHALLENGES OF POSTGRADUATE FIELDWORK 'AT HOME'

Uwem Ite

INTRODUCTION

Postgraduate research students wishing to contribute new knowledge and/or further the understanding of the major issues and debates in their fields are usually faced with the task of deciding on the spatial context of the research. For overseas students, especially those from developing countries, the choice of 'where' the fieldwork will be conducted could be a serious problem. In many cases, the decisions reached often result in the students having to go back 'home' for fieldwork. The mere thought of the 'trip' could sound thrilling and constitute a matter of tremendous excitement for the student. Possible reasons include, the rare opportunity to escape from the unreliability of the UK weather and a chance to prove to others that geography is not just about 'people and places', but that there is an element of 'doing geography' which culminates in trips or visits to these places to meet the people. It could also provide an avenue to demonstrate to fellow countrymen and women, as well as friends engaged in laboratory- or library-based research that geography really matters in the modern world. Yet the challenges and perils of such an adventure at home if overlooked, could work against the realisations of the lofty aims and objectives of the proposed research programme.

This chapter highlights some of the challenges of undertaking postgraduate fieldwork 'at home' from the perspective of an overseas student from a developing country registered for a Geography PhD in the UK. It is based on selective reflection of my experiences as a research student at Cambridge (UK) undertaking fieldwork at home (Nigeria) on the role of small farmers in tropical moist forest loss, and the impact of forest conservation on farmers in the Cross River National Park (CRNP) in south-eastern Nigeria.

FIELDWORK AT HOME: TRANSFORMING VISION TO ACTION

The translation of the visions of fieldwork at home into fruitful action can pose several challenges which are explored below.

Why home? The theoretical framework selected for any research is meant to guide the understanding of the processes and patterns of events and phenomena over time and space. For example, the use of the concept of political ecology to understand tropical forest loss in Cross River State could also be applied to the Brazilian Amazon. However, the choice of whether the work should be focused on Nigeria or Brazil can be influenced by several non-academic factors, including family commitments and relationships, funding limitations, safety, and prior knowledge of the area. In general, there is no doubt that there are immense hidden advantages in undertaking fieldwork in your home country. Nonetheless, it can be a shaky strategy if the fieldwork location cannot be sufficiently justified on academic grounds.

In the course of providing a sharper academic focus and practical relevance of my research, it was evident that the World Conservation Monitoring Centre (WCMC), Cambridge and the World Wide Fund for Nature (WWF-UK), Godalming were very interested in the potential findings, especially in relation to Nigeria. As a result, both the WCMC and WWF-UK offered to provide most of the background technical information about the Cross River National Park, as well as further contacts (mostly in conservation circles) in Nigeria. Within Nigeria, many organisations and establishments (e.g. Federal Surveys Department, Cross River Forestry Department, Cross River Agricultural Development Project) were willing to help in the research, although with some reservations. These made the choice of Nigeria as the main research base more attractive, in academic terms, than going to Brazil.

Being Nigerian helped in the research process. For one, it enabled me to appreciate the bureaucratic processes of the civil service and to approach their personnel differently than I would have done in the UK to get similar assistance. For example, the Federal Survey Department were initially uneasy in providing the aerial photos for the study area since it had a common boundary with the Cameroon. Being Nigerian helped to speed up the formal application and acquisition process for the photos. Ethnic links within the Department made possible the submission, processing and approval of my application for the purchase of the photos within four hours. Normally (I was told) this would have taken up to two weeks if not more. Nonetheless, it is not immediately clear to extent to which such assistance would have been extended to a foreigner. Indeed, it might be a case of who you know rather than who and what you are.

Where at home? Research can be conceived and conducted at different spatial scales. Once the question 'Why home?' has been adequately justified, the problem still remains of the choice of the actual site or field area. It might be tempting to leave it 'until I get there', thinking 'after all it's my country' or 'I know the area and the people very well'. However, experience shows that this could be counter-productive. Within the context of my study (Ite, 1995), there were two possibilities: the south-west and the south-east of Nigeria. The limitations of time and financial resources precluded a study of both regions. However, two main reasons guided the decision to focus the research on tropical moist forests of the south-east. Firstly, when the study was initiated in September/October 1992, the political climate of Nigeria was highly unstable.[1] The initial research plan was to focus in detail on hunting in protected areas, a sensitive topic. I would have been a non-indigene in the western states of Nigeria, hence it was felt that my safety and the progress of the research could be at risk. It was hoped that the problems would be reduced in south-east Nigeria - a region that was politically calm. Thankfully, it remained so throughout the duration of the fieldwork.

Secondly, following a preliminary visit in March/April 1993, the research proposal was revised. This revised plan involved a study of small farmers, their use of the forest environment, and the relationship between local people and external conservation project interventions. The Cross River National Park, the first tropical moist forest national park in Nigeria, presented an excellent opportunity to do this. Within the boundaries of the CRNP, the Okwangwo District was chosen. Preliminary discussions of the research proposal in September-October 1992 with tropical conservation practitioners and organisations in the UK (e.g. WCMC and WWF) strongly indicated that little was known about resource use and conservation in this area. It was hoped that the proposed study would make a useful contribution to filling the information gaps necessary for better management of the National Park. Thus, these considerations provided the main driving force for undertaking fieldwork at home (Nigeria), not abroad (Brazil).

---

[1] See Chapter 10 for further discussion of fieldwork and political instability.

'YES! I'M GOING HOME FOR FIELDWORK'

The decision to proceed home for fieldwork may not be easy, although it may be an exciting prospect. There are many questions to answer on arrival:

'Welcome to the village, but who are you?'

Your arrival in the study area is probably the first time you will be meeting the people who may turn out to benefit from your PhD research. A pertinent issue is your identity and people's perceptions of you as the new arrival (see also Elsbeth Robson's chapter). The 'identity kit' comprises your state or local government area, home town or village of origin in the country, as well as your links with and in the UK. Although you are unlikely to need a birth certificate to satisfy the requirements of the former, for the latter, a UK university ID card, or letter from your research supervisor can be very useful. However, the danger is that such documents could be misinterpreted, thereby raising expectations. For example, the letter of general introduction from my college tutor in Cambridge clearly stated among other things, that I was on a scholarship. In the Okwangwo villages most people interpreted this to meant that I was rich and laden with foreign currency, which when converted into the Nigerian currency would make me a rich man by local standards. It was obvious that most people were happy to be associated with me and my work with the hope of benefiting financially during my sojourn in the villages. A particular case in point was in one village where there was a dispute as to who should provide me with accommodation. The head chief fell out with a member of his executive council after I decided to change 'base' from the chief's residence. Most members of the community attributed this to the greed on the part of the chief, who normally had the privilege of hosting and benefiting (in cash and kind) from overseas-based researchers and visitors to the village. This incident nearly jeopardised the success of the research in this particular village.

Ideally, your identity should communicate appropriate messages about you as an individual, and also your mission in the study area. However, this is rarely the case as your research is bound to touch on a number of issues, the responses to which will be given against the background of whether you are perceived as an 'outsider' or an 'insider' in the system, and/or sometimes both. In my experience in the villages of the Mbe Mountains complex, for example, most members of the communities could not understand why I, given the chance to reside abroad, had decided to return to Nigeria and live nowhere else but the villages, just to ask questions about bananas, gorillas and the forest.

Despite the above, it is fair to say that I felt more of an insider than an outsider within the study villages, except for the language barrier. This assertion is based of the fact that I am a Nigerian, from Akwa Ibom State created in 1987 from the original Cross River State. I have lived in a rural area in my home state and can identify with many aspects rural livelihood (e.g. farming as the main occupation) and problems (e.g. lack of electricity). Nonetheless, it has to be acknowledged that these notions of fixed and correct identities within the context of research are hard to define and operationalise.

Although the fact that I was Nigerian was not disputed for a moment, there were many speculations as to my mission. There is no doubt that villagers' perceptions were based on fear, and some level of expectation. Most had the impression that I was sent personally by HRH Prince Philip the Duke of Edinburgh (the International President of the World Wide Fund for Nature) to assess the Park project after his earlier visit in 1989. It was thought that their appeal for better treatment by the park management had finally reached the Duke, hence his decision to send me to study their problems. Concerning hunting, most locals were initially afraid I was a secret agent for the National Park and would not, therefore, report cases of continued poaching, assuming they admitted to such practices. On the other hand, responses to questions on banana trading strongly suggested there was some level of expectation that I would be able to assist in enhancing the value-added of the produce. I was specifically requested to recommend a banana-based fruit drink industry in the area to enhance the socio-economic development.

Generally, although I received a warm welcome in the villages on arrival, I was sometimes perceived as an outsider (from the UK) and/or and insider (Nigerian) depending on the questions I was asking and the answers I provided to theirs. Responses to some questions on hunting (a sensitive issue) were provided based on their perception of me as an outsider (from the UK, or a Park secret agent), while those on banana trading reflected more of my being seen as an insider (Nigerian, probably with connections in high places). This had implications for the research findings. A particular case in point being my inability to undertake a full-scale hunting survey, or to gather much information on hunting income since I was perceived as an outsider in matters of such a sensitive nature. The challenge in this setting was to ensure being seen from only the best possible perspective within the research context. Again, this is difficult to operationalise.

'So why are you here? What have you got for us?'

Assuming that the hurdles resulting from the identity and perception crisis have been crossed, and perhaps cleared (although never permanently), there is a need to explain continuously the purpose and expected benefits of the research results in a bid to engender and sustain local support and co-operation for the research. This can be a formidable challenge, especially if the community has been exposed to other researchers from your country, who perhaps left the village empty promises of development. In this case, how different are you from those who had already been there?

There could be a situation whereby there are considerable variations in the extent to which different members of the community understand and appreciate the complex details of the research. It is from this that hopes are built, or despair is allowed to creep in, depending on the subject of the research. The challenge is to present a consistent explanation taking into account these anticipated variations, the possibility of positive, as well as negative opinions of the study, and the general implications of the findings. In my experience, the younger people had more understanding of my mission and were very critical of the rationale behind my research in their communities. Other members of the communities were curious as to the potential benefits of the research to their households in particular, and the villages in general. For example, during an early morning meeting in one village where I was explaining my research goals and potential benefits, one man openly opposed the continuation of research in the village. His opposition was based on the grounds that too many 'people' had been allowed to study bits and pieces about the community in relation to the National Park, yet nothing was accruing to the community in the form of development. He contended that since I was not an indigene of Boki land of Cross River State in the first place, it was more likely that nothing useful would accrue from my research in terms of socio-economic development in the village. The full weight of his criticism did not sink in immediately because he was speaking the local (Boki) language which I could not understand, but it was translated to me later.

'Eh! Sorry, but what did you say? I/We don't understand you'

There is the further challenge of a language barrier if the researcher does not speak nor understand the local language. The people in my study area are from Cross River State, while I am from Akwa Ibom State as mentioned earlier. *Boki* is the main (first) language spoken in the area, while my mother tongue is *Ibibio*. My mastery and understanding of *Boki* was poor by any local standard. English was the only option for the purposes of communication, yet it was necessary to interview elderly members of the community who spoke little or no English. The challenge here was to interpret the questions from English to Boki (invariably through an interpreter) and the reverse translation of responses into English for recording, without losing vital information. The fact that I was Nigerian and from the south eastern part of the country did not, in anyway help matters here. It was plain and simple: we could not understand each other without using English.[2]

TO AVOID THE PERILS, RISE ABOVE THE CHALLENGES

The preceding section has highlighted three main, yet interrelated challenges facing postgraduates study overseas, but undertaking fieldwork in their home countries: insider/outsider identities, the questions of local benefits from the research, and language barriers. The following section will attempt to offer some insights toward negotiating these and other challenges.

'But I'm from...'

Even if you are carrying out research 'at home' a preliminary visit to your study area is recommended for a number of reasons. Consider these scenarios: firstly, you may not be an indigene of the specific study area; secondly, you might have only visited the area some time ago, perhaps during your high school or an undergraduate geography excursion; and thirdly, you may only have been driven through the area en route to the international airport a few hours before your departure to the UK. Whatever your degree of familiarity with the research location, it is important to note that your perception, identification and articulation of the research issues or problem are likely to change significantly after the theoretical framework has been chosen and literature reviewed while in the UK. Therefore, initial and less formal interaction with the people of the area would assist in identifying potential problems, such as language, transport, local politics, food, water sources and availability, among other issues. This preliminary visit, if well utilised, can be the key to survival and success in the places which could possibly become 'home' away from the real home and/ or your college room in the UK. My preliminary site visit to the Okwangwo Division of the CRNP in March/April 1993 provided a different perspective of the research under review and further paved the way for the smooth running of the main field visit of June 1993 to March 1994.

---

[2] See also Sarah Howard's and Elsbeth Robson's chapters for a discussion of issues surrounding use of interpreters in fieldwork.

'Did I say that? When?'

The challenge of engendering and sustaining the best possible perception of you and the research is a formidable one. The best way of dealing with this problem is consistency concerning your identity, your mission and role towards resolving a particular problem. It is unethical and unwise to take advantage of local perceptions which do not fit with the goals of the research in order to acquire information. Since data collection during fieldwork is a two-way process, it is pertinent to stress here that local perceptions are bound to be ever-changing depending on the questions posed by the researcher. However, with time, local perceptions of the researcher and the research might possibly become steady and fixed, again depending on the level of consistency maintained in the process of answering questions from the population under study.

For example, my questions on the nature of the relationship between the people and the National Park led to initial local perceptions of my mission in the Mbe Mountains complex as someone sent by HRH Prince Philip to assess the management and operation of the Park. My earlier insistence of having never even spoken or met the Duke was taken with a pinch of salt. However, this changed a few weeks later when I was thought to be a 'secret agent' for the park management because I probed into household hunting activities, species hunted and income patterns. Thankfully, before long I was accurately known and addressed in the villages as 'that boy from Uyo, Akwa Ibom studying in the United Kingdom'.

'This is wrong. It cannot be done in Europe'

You are supposed to be a student, not judge or a teacher. The fact that you had the privilege to study abroad can provide a sense of elevation in social status and the tendency for the community to look up to, or keep away from, you in many ways. The challenge of establishing rapport and a good working relationship with the communities lies in objectivity and open-mindedness. Perhaps, the foremost way in this regard is to analyse why things are done the way they are from the communities' perspective. No matter how tempting the situation might be, it is better not to pass judgement and advocate change in village life and processes, even in the face of pressure from local community interest groups. Questions are best asked from the perspective of a learner (student), which you are, and not a teacher or 'expert' from abroad. That way, more confidence and sense of trust is generated, with significant implications for your research.

Personal experience in South-eastern Nigeria suggested that community members largely perceived me as a student, an independent researcher, outsider in some issues and insider in others. This was probably due to a number of reasons including my great unwillingness to be seen as teacher or expert. For example, my opinion was sought concerning the arbitration of a long-standing boundary dispute between two neighbouring communities I was studying. As a geographer, an insider (Nigerian), and outsider (from UK) with interests in forests (an expert), I was expected to provide a much-needed contribution. Nonetheless, I politely and diplomatically declined and reserved my comments on the basis of lack of sufficient information from both parties.

Nonetheless, the price paid for demonstrations of 'willingness to learn' and perhaps experiment can be high without considerable forethought and contingency planning. For example, to increase my acceptance and integration in the villages I strongly resisted the temptation to have my drinking water boiled frequently. The periodic adventure of drinking 'untreated' water from the village streams constituted a health risk. On two separate occasions I was diagnosed with typhoid fever. Luckily this was near the end of my stay. To remain healthy and complete the study, I had to 'import' cartons of bottled spring water into the villages, something I had wanted to avoid completely. It was clear that most members of the community (especially my host) had expected me to drink the local water. This would have been different with a foreigner. Again, the fact that I was a Nigerian, doing fieldwork at home did not help matters. I could have still caught typhoid if I had gone to Brazil and drank water of questionable quality.

CONCLUSIONS

Fieldwork at home, from the perspective of an overseas student from a developing country can be a two-edged sword, with thrills and perils. On the one hand, it can be of considerable advantage to the student in terms of proper knowledge of the political, social, cultural and economic conditions. This can enhance the collection of good quality data, and generate sustained interest in the research on the part of researcher and the researched. On the other hand, the perils of such an exercise derive mainly from laying the foundations of the research against the background of unrealistic assumptions and associated expectations. This might stem from the feeling of knowing much about the area prior to the fieldwork. As noted earlier, this is self-defeating as establishing the theoretical framework of the research is likely to provide a significant change of perspective of the research problem.

In general it is a great challenge to undertake fieldwork successfully at home (see, for example, Amadiume, 1993). Students face economic, political, cultural and social pressures and considerations which can work for or against them due to their nationality, and the way these attributes feed into the research process. A number of actions can help ameliorate these problems: firstly, you should consider the objectives and expected contributions of the chosen field of study. Secondly, draw up a realistic fieldwork plan indicating specific activities, timing, detailed objectives/ targets, critical assumptions and indicators of achievement of each component of the plan. Thirdly, consider how the economic, political, cultural and social attributes of the country in general, and the peculiarities of the specific study area will influence the success of the proposed project. Fourthly, and finally, while being prepared to adapt your studies in the field, try and stick to a basic timetable, bearing in mind that any lack of self-discipline and control in terms of time and resources could lead to either an extension of the fieldwork duration, or a complete deviation from, or abandonment of the research.

REFERENCES
Amadiume, Ifi 1993 'The mouth that spoke a falsehood will later speak the truth: Going home to the field in Eastern Nigeria', Bell, Diane, Caplan, Pat and Karim, Wazir Jahan (eds) Gendered Fields: Women, Men and Ethnography Routledge, London, 182-198.

Ite, Uwem E. 1995 'Agricultural Forest Conservation in Southeast Nigeria'. Unpublished PhD Dissertation, University of Cambridge, UK.

6.

ALTERNATIVE AFFILIATIONS AND THE PERSONAL POLITICS OF OVERSEAS RESEARCH: SOME REFLECTIONS[1]

Simon Batterbury

INTRODUCTION

In one of his best known essays, Clifford Geertz (1984) describes to us the extreme disquiet in anthropological circles occasioned by the publication of Malinowski's *A Diary in the Strict Sense of the Term* (1967). One of the world's leading anthropologists this century, Malinowski's previous ethnographic work had been highly praised for its richness and detail and had served as a model of sound fieldwork practice. But in his contentious diary, the author laid bare his real feelings towards his island hosts, had 'rude words' to say about them, and divulged that he spent much of his time while in the field "wishing he was elsewhere" and "preoccupied with his own well-being" (Hammersley & Atkinson 1983, 101).

According to Geertz, the impact of the book was far-reaching; had some been too hasty in venerating Malinowski? Does all fieldwork involve selfish sentiment and introspection, and was this simply the first instance of a major author owning up to his own shortcomings in this regard? In any event, the effect of publication was that,

"The myth of the chameleon fieldworker, perfectly tuned to his exotic surroundings, a walking miracle of empathy, tact, patience and cosmopolitanism, was demolished by the man who had perhaps done most to create it" (Geertz 1983, 56).

[1] These reflections are based on 17 months of doctoral fieldwork spent with the Mossi of Bam, Burkina Faso in 1992-3. I gratefully acknowledge funding from a Social Science Research Council 'FTDR' doctoral fellowship in African Agriculture, the assistance of GTZ's PATECORE project, and the support and advice of the Graduate School community at Clark University. I would like to thank Tony Bebbington, Sue Buckingham-Hatfield, Patricia Meono-Picado, Mike Turner and the editors for comments.

Another observer of anthropological culture, James Clifford, later marked the event thus; "Henceforth an implicit mark of interrogation was placed beside any overly confident and consistent ethnographic voice" (Clifford 1986).

Using a discussion of Malinowski's honest account of his personal foibles and ingratitude as a basis, Geertz goes on to construct his own argument about the problems of grasping 'native' understanding in fieldwork settings more generally. He therefore refuses to take Malinowski's journal for what it is - discomfort with 'other' landscapes and cultures. For Geertz, good interpretative anthropology in alien environments does not involve complete immersion in local culture, nor the maintenance of strict 'social distance' between researcher and researched. Both positions may be problematic for the researcher (see Hammersley & Atkinson 1983, 93). In Geertz's view the observer should strive towards a more authentic working position where s/he is able to tack between local detail (the 'exotic minutiae' of culture) and global structures of various forms (through 'sweeping characterisations' and attention to structural logic and causes), in such a way as to bring the key elements of *both* scales into view at the same time. Such an approach reveals the semiotic play that constructs that other self, and is most likely to yield ethnographic richness and a 'thick' - careful and detailed - description of local culture. C. Wright Mills hinted at a similar position in his passionate incitement to sociology. For Mills, the sociological imagination is the "... capacity to range from the most interpersonal and remote transformations to the most intimate features of the self - and to see the relations between the two" (Mills 1959, 7).

Geertz concludes his article by suggesting that, despite his admitted imperfections, we still consider Malinowski an outstanding 'fieldworker' and interpreter of culture. For Geertz, a researcher's conduct and professionalism in the field is less important than an ability create 'thick descriptions'. One could paraphrase by saying that authorial blemishes are acceptable, *if* the methods employed are 'thick' and detailed and allow the 'figuring out' of behaviour and symbol systems. Despite the feelings he expressed about village life and local people in the Pacific Islands, ultimately it was Malinowski's ability to tack between scales and to construe modes of expression that sets him apart; an almost transcendental ability that Geertz likens to "grasping a proverb, catching an allusion, seeing a joke" (Geertz 1983, 70). Perhaps by confining his personal feelings to the pages of his journal, Malinowski was able to develop and refine his interpretative skill.

Other chapters in this volume, especially those by Sarah Howard, Uwem Ite, Clare Madge and Elsbeth Robson, explore ways to develop personal interpretative strategies in geographical fieldwork, and thus hint at some of these important debates over anthropological method and responsibility. In examining how their own personalities stood up to the assault on the senses of 'other' cultures and places, some of the contributors consider how this influenced the content and conduct of their research. Certainly, for geographers, Geertz's notion of 'tacking' between scales - of which the relationship between the intimate and the remote is exemplary - is an attractive one, particularly when linked to a vision of complexity in human-environment relations and of geographical relationships.

I will return to this issue later in the chapter, but want to note first that the challenge facing many potential fieldworkers is often a more immediate one; how to plan for and carry out fieldwork in the first place. Getting the research *done* involves not so much the drawing up and enactment of a research blueprint, but more the progressive unfurling of a tapestry of logistical hurdles, travel, waiting, funding difficulties, acquisition of new skills, the completion of exams and paperwork and a degree of personal fortitude. These constitute a sort of 'personal politics' of field research, or what Delamont (1992, 8) calls 'investigator effects'. They underpin and condition the circumstances under which the fieldwork takes place. In any research project it is vital not to ignore personal attributes and sentiments (of the sort shown in Malinowski's Diary). Pretending that one *can* only adds to the problem of interpreting other cultures.

This chapter frames the question of interpretation by offering some observations on fieldwork experience, and then goes on to suggest a way to position oneself such that the sort of cultural interpretation proposed by Geertz may flourish. To do this it is necessary to dwell on the problem of *finding and developing institutional affiliations* in the field, and to discuss how the prospects for doing detailed and relevant fieldwork are in no sense diminished - and may be improved - by exploring alternative alliances while in foreign countries. This argument reflects my own experiences working as a geographer within non-academic, practically oriented organisations in Africa. I wrote the piece because I believe certain sorts of applied research, perhaps more readily conducted outside the university, are valuable. Regretfully, some of these research avenues may be frowned upon by the discipline, or lack favour with funding bodies. Furthermore, it is evident that 'doing geography' is ultimately what David Mercer (1984) calls a 'political act', in that one's choice of research patronage and affiliation may not, and need not, be taken in innocence. Who geographers align and affiliate themselves with while in the field influences the entire process of fieldwork. We need to address this issue.

SELF-PRESENTATION

While re-reading Geertz's work, I could not help casting a suspicious eye towards my own weathered fieldwork diaries, for it is there that my own efforts towards 'thick description' are exposed along with documentation of anger, despair and occasional bouts of short-lived euphoria. An important point surfaced from this introspection, about how presentation influences all forms of ethnographic work.

The reverse side of understanding the construction of the self is how one presents oneself to the 'natives' (cf. Clifford 1986). This is important because the latter also interpret cultural signs coming from strangers in their society (Goffman 1959). During my own fieldwork in Mossi communities of Burkina Faso, I was constantly involved in self-presentation and my conscious and unconscious actions - greetings and departures, body positioning, clothing and appearance, as well as general social conduct and behaviour were closely observed. Indeed for any new arrival language, ethnicity, race, gender and indigenous estimates of your potential wealth and power unavoidably help define the subsequent course of social interaction and communication; these factors are vital considerations in any cross-cultural research project (Delamont 1992, 133; Francis 1992, 88; Katz 1994, 68).

But there is another issue at stake here, relevant to research conduct; namely, how the 'presentation of self', to use Goffman's (1959) famous phrase, is linked to other organisations and institutions known by local people to be active in a region. What sorts of links do people make between the researcher and such other organisations, as they attempt to locate, or place, a stranger in their midst? Who *is* the strange new arrival? What is this so-called student/project worker saying about her/his reasons for being here? What organisation is s/he with? Can s/he be trusted? Who owns his/her mode of transport - does it belong to a project, or did s/he have sufficient funds to buy it? For any researcher, these issues are particularly important since the outcome of such local deliberations will inevitably influence the future deployment of a research strategy and its success - local people will be attentive to the way you are introduced to them by other outsiders they already know. Furthermore, they will wish to know more about the conditions underlying your presence in a village in the first place - how much power do you wield, and do you merit special attention?

In my own case, suspicion of my presence in one especially remote village was much reduced, and the subsequent engagement with local people over many months made much more satisfactory, because of a pre-arranged affiliation with a functioning rural development organisation active in the region and known to the majority of rural people. My reasons for 'being there' were assessed not only through observation of my demeanour and conduct, but also through the linkage people made between the project and myself, for good or for bad. Katz (1994, 68) describes a similar experience in Sudan; she was introduced to a village by social workers from an agricultural project and this had both 'obvious and subtle' effects on her work. What could be termed the structural conditions of fieldwork (which include *organisational affiliations* and *reasons for being there*), then, provide the backdrop for such encounters. They permeate them.

This question of how a researcher's institutional affiliations influence presentation and the conduct of ethnographic work has received little discussion even in anthropology. Yet a voluminous literature now exists on the conduct and context of fieldwork and the subjectivity of ethnographic work has been analysed quite extensively (Barnes & Duncan 1992; Clifford & Marcus 1986; Delamont 1992; van Maanen 1988; see also the reading list at the end of this volume). The fundamental issue of *why* to conduct first-world to third-world fieldwork at all, and the significant moral implications this raises, has also been examined in some depth (Bebbington 1993, Deveraux & Hoddinott 1992, Nast & contributors 1994, Rogers 1991). Yet if affiliations form part of the 'presentation of self', a stated affiliation with an organisation (or group of individuals) encourages local people to attempt to 'glean clues' and divine an outsider's purpose. Locals will utilise what they already know about the organisation as a 'sign vehicle' (Goffman 1959, 1) guiding their assessment of the person, to locate their purpose more readily in an initial encounter, or perhaps to apply heard but untested stereotypes to them (Hammersley & Atkinson 1983, 77). Stated, or assumed, affiliations may confuse, or may improve, the communication process; they may provide efficient 'entry-points' to dialogue, but equally can lay one open to the same suspicion, or dissatisfaction, which coloured the community's previous dealings with your organisation. In simpler terms, they *influence* the research process, *disturb* power relations, and *permeate* everyday encounters.

Affiliations are also deeply implicated in what Norman Long terms an actor-oriented approach to rural development work and research. Actor approaches look at the relationships between the different players in development work, and their aim is to bring about "deconstruction of conventional notions of planned interventions" (Long 1992, 9). By understanding the cultural puzzles associated with development work, they investigate the viability, or effectiveness, of human rationales for solving specific social problems (Torres 1992, Ndione, et al 1995). Here, one's own affiliation (as a project staff member, consultant or student, for example) is extremely important. For those conducting research into development interventions, it is necessary to present oneself in such a way that allows rationales to be questioned and to interact *across* social groups - from the village to the extension agency, from the individual farmer to the development project, or the local state, and thereby to keep all of these groups in 'simultaneous view'. Combining Geertz's ethnographic richness with Long's sociological focus on human agents and institutions is fruitful, especially where researchers address practical issues in their own fieldwork. And for those who believe it is truly possible, one may be able to 'make a difference' in rural settings if working sensitively toward change and 'politically centred action' in and around a particular organisation, or community (Madge 1993, 297, but see Wilson 1992).

GEOGRAPHY

How are such issues treated in our own discipline? At least for the relatively small group of geographers pursuing long-term research in developing countries, who are still vastly outnumbered in the discipline (Potter 1993), one's affiliation does not seem to have been given the consideration it deserves. Few of these authors mention their own affiliations or their effects on social interaction and data collection. Sidaway comes close to initiating a debate when he suggests the "...social context, conditions and consequences" (Sidaway 1992, 404) of overseas fieldwork have been neglected in geography. The reasons for this lacuna are many, and it was instructive to hear the issue being debated with some feeling at the Nottingham IBG conference session (January 1994) from which the first edition of this volume derives.

Geographers, student or established, and of western and non-western origin, have their own tales to tell on the issue of research practice in non-western settings. Creativity may be required to circumvent funding problems, or visa restrictions, particularly in a shrinking market for conventionally-funded postgraduate study in geography. Referring to good research practice in developing countries, Sidaway suggests the "...ideal answer is for us to be involved in collaborative and mutually co-operative research led by the host country but this is not always possible" (Sidaway 1992, 405). Yet while he cautions that all research be made available and conducted with the knowledge of national institutions, he seems opposed to those who attach themselves to development aid projects in particular. If taken at face value, this is puzzling, especially when there are now professional associations devoted to research on the sociology of development projects as 'change agents'.[2] The urgent question raised is this; are we simultaneously to salute the emancipatory potential of certain forms of projects (NGOs, for example) in promoting positive social and environmental change (Bebbington & Thiele 1993, Clark 1991, Friedmann 1992), and yet confine our research linkages to more distant academic vistas, or to the public sphere alone? Can we not be free to work across the range of grassroots organisations, NGOs, bilateral programmes and research institutes as well as in universities and with government departments? Do we not have something to contribute to all of these, and can we not work with them?

Perhaps geographers are afraid of self-criticism in this regard, although it is true that several individuals have already been engaged in more practically oriented projects. A considerable diversity exists in the ways that postgraduate geographers are able to conduct fieldwork. A postgraduate project may be strongly linked to a supervisor's own research, or contacts; in this case the student may have little choice in the matter of field location, or affiliation. Alternatively, there may be a university field office fully equipped to manage student projects, with facilities and projects already in place. Operating from such centres may render initial encounters with local communities easier, if the student simply joins an ongoing research programme, for example. Wageningen Agricultural University maintains an impressive *Antenne Sahelienne* in Ouagadougou, West Africa; its students may use this centre, and its existing projects, as bases for their own work. Several geography departments (Durham University geography department, for example) have long-standing arrangements with universities in developing countries for exchanges and research work.

Yet for the majority of postgraduates, simple practicalities mean seeking a link to a similar institution to their own when in the field. The national, or regional university, and its geography department, is often the first port of call. Such a concrete academic link seems to be the type preferred by funding bodies like the ESRC, and the equally influential Social Science Research Council and National Science Foundation in the USA; all three are cautious about allowing students to strike out (cash in hand) into uncharted waters without suitable affiliations and prior research permissions.

---

[2] For example, APAD (association euro-africaine pour l'anthropologie du changement social et du développement), run by JP Olivier de Sardan and Thomas Bierschenk - see Section 13 for address, and DARG Newsletter No. 25, Autumn 1996 for further details.

Yet other options do exist. French and German geographers are frequently contracted as research assistants to specific projects, or conduct their research from the sanctity of government research bodies, such as ORSTOM for the French; or a project office of the GTZ (German technical assistance organisation). Students of tropical geography at Bayreuth, Berlin, Göttingen, Hohenheim, Montpellier and Frankfurt Universities are well placed to pursue these options. A minority wish to remain totally independent, eschew all links except for those necessary to satisfy the local authorities, and head off to field sites to grapple first-hand with local culture unshackled by bureaucracy or support networks. Lastly, some students use their own ethnic, or cultural position, to adopt a partial 'insider' perspective, working in their own ethnic, or social group, and this brings its own theoretical and practical difficulties (Byron 1993, Ite, this volume, Razavi 1992). The possibilities in postgraduate research are therefore numerous.

In my own case I was a decided 'outsider' with an interest in understanding and contributing to locally managed efforts to halt Sahelian land degradation. A busy, field-based rural development project seemed the most appropriate local affiliation and I was fortunate to work in a region where NGOs and development projects are relatively numerous. My project link came about because I felt intuitively that I was witnessing the 'front line' of environmental activism and a passion for rural concerns in and around the organisation, which I wanted to observe in the fashion of 'action research'. The commitment I observed among staff of the project contrasted strongly with the rather distanced manner of university-based academics I had previously met in the capital city (see discussion of this problem in Peil 1982).

ALTERNATIVE AFFILIATIONS?

Indulging in non-conventional or applied research always brings risks with it, if it challenges professional hierarchies. It may also require some courage to set in motion, as I will suggest in closing this chapter. Yet it is still the case that the diversity of ways in which students can conduct their fieldwork, as set out in the previous section, represent a number of what we may call 'alternative' affiliations and research strategies. Looking specifically at postgraduate research, it is clear that some geography students have explored diverse options in their overseas fieldwork. Far from confining themselves to the strictures of funding bodies, or supervisors' advice, students are *already* interacting and working with a range of organisations and institutions, which past and future students can learn from them. Some 'alternative' affiliations are openly declared in written output, others, for political or personal reasons, remain concealed. Here I merely present a few alternative approaches, and comment briefly on their implications.

Development Projects

From grassroots support organisations to international NGOs, development projects have research needs. NGOs are particularly eclectic in their methods and aims, but if they exist in one's field area, they should not be dismissed when looking around for affiliations, or contacts. They frequently operate in remote rural areas in which consultancy teams, or academics, may be unwilling to spend much time. However, they are nonetheless in daily contact with rural people and actively valorising a particular vision of environmental, or social, change. They can also welcome the occasional researcher, provided their rules are respected and demands not made on staff who may be overburdened with other duties and administration. For example, a small NGO in northern Ghana called TRAX has been running basic soil and water conservation programmes for six years, expanding over that time to work in at least eight villages. Staffed by a handful of British and Ghanaian workers, all on volunteer salaries, a lack of time and money had prevented any detailed research assessment of their environmental programme. When a student made contact wishing to study indigenous use of tree species and later arrived at the project field office, the field director expressed an interest in the proposed research, and was able to offer basic support for six months work. The research output - a dossier of tree crops and their uses - was fed back into project activities as an aid to extension work and for a tree nursery, as well as being later written up as a thesis. This is an example of applied research, occasioned by an informal contact and done cheaply, which was valorised locally in a modest organisation far removed from a top-down development 'aid' setting.

A further example comes from Burkina Faso, where the well-known OXFAM-supported *Projet Agro-Forestier* (PAF) project has hosted very informal research contacts since its inception in 1979. Roche's (1984) little-known study of cereal grain banks was conducted with a Dudley Stamp research award, and used intensive fieldwork and household surveys to analyse the efficacy of community grain banks for OXFAM and for the local administration. Two of the most fruitful studies linked to the project have revolved around evaluating the efficiency of locally developed soil and water conservation techniques, and on conceptions of participation and local accountability in the project. Rather than examining these issues though expensive outside consultants, students (both, as it turned out, with prior NGO/volunteer experience in the region) were supported in their own research endeavours.

Jonathan Hooper provided a quantitative assessment on the suitability of stone bunds for soil fertility enhancement and erosion control on certain soil types. His M.Sc. thesis (Hooper 1989) contained simple summaries and photographs, and copies were lodged with OXFAM and with institutions in Ouagadougou; it permitted an appraisal of the soil conservation techniques promoted by the project. Peter Gubbels, an experienced NGO worker on leave for postgraduate study, conducted research on the effective participation of land users in PAF's environmental work, spending several weeks examining the issue both from the village and the project office (Gubbels 1993). Similarly, his M.A. thesis (Gubbels 1992) has been of particular interest to the project, exposing the limitations inherent in the unique 'bottom-up' approach to land use planning guiding PAF's programme. Gubbel's former organisation, World Neighbours, has also hosted overseas students conducting basic research, and has a new research strategy linked to its practical programmes.

These examples are not uncommon in smaller development organisations. What unites the cases above is the emphasis on valorising knowledge *within* the organisation and thus, in *applying* it (perhaps after the student has left) to the local area. An NGO's funding or time restrictions may have prevented such research from being carried out by staff, or consultants, in the past. Such opportunities for practical research links *do* exist. Many key British-based NGOs including ACORD, SOS Sahel and Action Aid have active research programmes. In many cases, striking personal rapport with individuals at their workplaces, or in casual meetings, can lead to the offer of a project visit, a research trip, or less commonly some help with visas, or financial support - the latter can never be assumed and should not be pushed for. To arrange such linkages is not as costly, or as difficult, as many would believe. Outlays may be involved for travel to the area and for setting up the research, but it is often one's physical presence in the field - confident, ready and willing to work - that can secure interest and an offer of closer collaboration. In some cases, arranging one's own funding is vital, but minimal research expenses may sometimes be paid. Working with such projects can be intensely satisfying, since one is visibly 'giving something back' in a defined way. It is regrettable that such 'applied' and 'engaged' work of this nature is poorly recognised in the academy (cf. Katz 1994, 71, but see Breheny 1989).

Bilateral Programmes and International Aid Organisations
It is not unusual for enterprising students to be offered research contracts to carry out specific pieces of work with bilateral projects, or larger aid organisations. Such arrangements are increasingly common, particularly in the continental European countries and in the USA (where postgraduate 'teaching assistantships' rarely cover overseas fieldwork costs). Geographers and their ilk can profit from the new climate of accountability now permeating such organisations and the international 'development business' more widely. While the large donors and projects have poorer reputations among academic researchers, they can offer significant alternatives to university affiliations, especially in parts of the world where universities have few links. One cannot deny their influence; so working with them affords opportunities to test preconceived notions of organisational behaviour and ethics, and perhaps to initiate change too. It is vital, however, to retain objectivity, ethical diligence (Wilson 1988, 184) and a sense of perspective while working with the larger well-funded bodies, as previous students have done.

For example, a student registered for a British Ph.D. and with experience in forestry conducted a year of innovative fieldwork in West Africa on women's tree crops, funded entirely by a research contract with GTZ (German technical assistance organisation). She enjoyed better support in the field and for the write-up period than an ESRC studentship, or equivalent award, could provide. Critical in this case was a link forged with a German university, with whom the research was developed. Over several years in West Africa I have met many students who had been able to negotiate similar arrangements. Often, it was precisely the lack of prior attention to detailed field-level research (and a dissatisfaction with hastily prepared consultant evaluations) that had convinced policy makers to take a student on. While continuing to receive a bad press from its critics, USAID disburses funds for student research done in collaboration with national research institutions, for example on targeting agricultural technologies to farmers, or to assess the potential of intercropping systems for enhanced food security. ODA offers similar opportunities through its competitive overseas training schemes. Such research, if well presented and of applied value, may feed its way into project activities in positive ways.

Of course such organisations have their own designs at heart, although students should be able to resist entrapment in sponsor's power politics (Wilson 1992). It is important to bear in mind what sort of impact the affiliation may have on local perceptions of you the researcher, and whether there will be freedom to pursue an individual line of research which permits critique and reflection. It is unfortunate if the organisation is unpopular in the host region, perhaps because of the way its previous interventions have been conducted. Projects with a record of problems, or even failure to meet their objectives, may be quite anxious to enlist young social researchers (or cartographers and land-use specialists) to help them 'target' project activities more effectively in the future and to show donors that serious research is underway in the area. A lucrative research stipend, easy access to field locations, and a rapid route through bureaucratic hurdles will never compensate for a sullen reception in the village, or the imposition of unreasonable report submission dates, or even restrictions on report content.

A key issue to look into is the extent to which an international programme intervenes directly at the local level, or alternatively if it works primarily through existing government services, or local agencies. The latter situation offers more latitude for 'doing your own thing' and working with nationals, since the philosophy of the organisation does not permit it to operate quite as openly in the field with expensive vehicles, technical apparatus and expatriate staff.

My own affiliation in Burkina Faso was with a German-funded bilateral programme of the latter local type. I discuss here some of the 'presentational' and practical issues associated with this research environment, since they illustrate some of the points made in preceding sections. I believe the affiliation was beneficial in several ways; certainly it aided my ethnographic encounters and the formulation of 'thick' interpretations of the knowledge systems and development activities I was observing. Certain of these insights may have been closed off had I been working in a more conventional academic environment. Not only was the project largely staffed by nationals, it was also well respected by land users prior to my arrival. But I worked alone in villages, or with one assistant, and took care to set out my links to the project very carefully at all stages of the research. A willingness to wait, and to be flexible over the research proposal facilitated the initial offer of affiliation and eased the required research permissions. I was able to participate in village environmental activities as an individual, but also to accompany project staff in the field, observe and monitor their actions, and to work with them if I wished to do so (for example on demonstration plots for soil and water conservation, in rapid rural appraisal exercises, or as a 'link person' to a particularly remote area where much of the research was conducted).

In this way, the affiliation - while not of an academic nature - was vital to my understanding of both the structure of rural life, and the practical activities of the project and those like it. It is interesting that villagers did not seem puzzled over the seeming contradiction in my status (a student, or a project worker?), viewing me as independent but 'linked' to the project somehow. This perception of my dual status only became evident during the course of rapid appraisal exercises conducted later in one village (IIED/PATECORE 1993). It emerged that in many instances individual farmers, engaged in their own symbolic struggles, believed they had much to gain from speaking honestly to me, 'the project researcher', about agricultural practices and household welfare (Batterbury 1996). They did this *because of my affiliation*, without that link, I would have been just another visitor asking questions. In my current research project in southwestern Niger, I am just that: I have no affiliation, and I have found there to be great confusion over my project and its purpose.

Nonetheless, having a local affiliation in Burkina Faso did not in itself permit complete and open communication. I also had to prove that, despite my whiteness and gender, I was not a fleeting visitor or a well-off expatriate with access to what René Dumont (1986) calls the three V's - 'villas, voitures, voyages'. Individuals responded more openly about their economic situations when this became clear, thus demonstrating to me the importance of the range of 'self-presentation' issues discussed above. It was important to keep these in mind in other settings. In the project itself, expatriate students were placed low in the pecking order and were required to defer to higher authority at all times. This forced a useful perspective and a certain social distance on us. Yet research could, to a limited extent, be 'applied', or put into practice locally. This was usually done through reporting back to project staff and discussing their future interventions in the field area in the light of my own experience with 'marginal' and distant social groups that they themselves had not contacted. Being able to 'float' in diverse social settings and between many actors - whether one takes on the role of advocate or not - is a challenging but ultimately rewarding way to do and to valorise research. This is the key lesson to emerge in my own case, and my affiliation eased and underpinned this social and personal positioning. I return to this point in the conclusion, since I believe it to be a valid strategy for doctoral work as well as for other research projects.

International Agricultural Research Organisations
A small number of geographers have successfully conducted long-term fieldwork based within, or around, international or government research centres (for a review, see Bebbington & Carney 1990). These organisations are concerned with the development of new agricultural practices and technologies, and less with hands-on development activities. Research student collaborations with them is rare, since it is particularly noticeable that the theoretical elaborations of academic researchers are not always welcome (Bebbington 1993, 155). Even once installed there, some students find the requirements of doctoral study may not mesh with the more pragmatic, or applied, research needs of the institution. Yet such links are not unknown, and post-doctoral schemes exist to bring researchers to these organisations after graduate study; geographers including Abe Goldman, Dianne Rocheleau, Matthew Turner and Judy Carney have participated in these before beginning an academic career (Bebbington & Carney 1990).

For example, Bebbington's (1990) work in Ecuador and Peru was conducted with the International Potato Center and a national agricultural research organisation, and demonstrates that, with care, applied and relevant research can be carried out within the context of higher-level research organisations of this sort. Indeed, despite their anti-theory stance, staff of such institutions, who are often deprived of the time and the opportunity to read and reflect outside their area of expertise, can find contact with academic researchers instructive and challenging. This can be mutually enriching, or can lead to other research avenues later. Bebbington's study, while partly of a theoretical nature, helped answer a local need for baseline research in Ecuador and was followed up with a local NGO over a five year period. It has since led to the generation of several applied research projects on NGO-state relations in other countries (e.g. Bebbington & Thiele 1993).

Among the international agricultural research stations (generally termed the CGIAR centres) involved in crop research, certain institutes, including IRRI, CIP, CIAT and ICRISAT, are well known for the opportunities afforded to postgraduate students (but not necessarily geographers), who are often taken on as temporary research staff on reasonable local stipends. Fairhead, an anthropologist, describes his arrangement with CIAT's bean improvement programme in Zaire as a 'semi-formal ad-hoc co-operation' in which he acted as a sort of cultural 'broker' in a project already dedicated to farmer participation in agricultural research (Fairhead 1993, 188). Not all collaborations may be as potentially fruitful. But it is often possible to 'turn up' at such institutions, initially for research visits, or through pre-arranged personal contacts, and to explore research possibilities directly once there. Unfortunately, expatriates often can receive more favourable terms of support than students from developing countries, although this is not always so.

Bebbington sees a particular 'hermeneutic advantage' to affiliation with a known and trusted international, or national, research centre, which parallels my own situation in a development project; in initial village encounters, the 'foreign' researcher is something of a known quantity, 'placed' and understood, not a complete stranger who arrives unsupported and talks of questionnaires, understanding local culture, or scientific measurements (see section on self-presentation above). While affiliation linkages like this may of course lead to biases, they are highly appropriate if one's research hinges in any way on conceptions of agrarian change, sustainability and agricultural policy, in which agricultural research centres are deeply implicated in certain parts of the world (Bebbington & Carney 1990, 42). It is unfortunate that links between research institutes and the non-governmental organisations referred to above are often weak. A review of NGO and research institutes links for Burkina Faso notes that "...the findings of research institutes have practically no effect on NGO activity as a result of the lack of co-operation between the two types of agency" (Lindskog & Mando 1992, 15). This raises the question, not addressed in detail here, of whether it may be possible to link both sorts of institutions in field research.

Volunteer Networks

It is unusual, though not impossible, to conduct a research project while working as a volunteer. The idea is an attractive one, particularly for those unable to secure research funds in other ways, but only works if entered into with a serious commitment and where one has genuine skills to offer. Basic research may be possible while working in rural settings, although pay levels rarely permit grand projects. Serious research has actually been done by several French volunteers working on long-term agricultural change in West Africa, and by the occasional teacher stationed overseas, but it would be unwise to suggest the possibility of joining a volunteer service such as UNAIS, or VSO, only *in order* to conduct research. The volunteer organisations themselves would be likely to see through this in any event. But the aims of volunteer organisations and practically oriented researchers, could coalesce in certain instances. Much of the work reported by Toulmin (1992) was undertaken as part of a research inquiry into agro-pastoral livelihood systems, staffed by UNAIS volunteers who spent long periods in the field (see also Ayers 1992, a volunteer study of NGO performance in Bolivia). UNAIS supported a Dutch forestry student in central Burkina Faso, who provided technical advice to a very small

NGO agroforestry programme. This individual was in a position to collect data and to write reports on the performance of tree crops and farmer management.

Rather than conduct scholarly research while volunteering, it has been more common for returnee volunteers to go back to the same region later as research students and many ex-volunteers return to further study. A sizeable number of students conducting overseas-based research in some of the more 'difficult' countries and registered in doctoral programmes in U.S. universities were once Peace Corps volunteers; returning to 'their' areas, they have significant advantages of local knowledge and language competence, and tend to be less socially distanced than students undertaking their first visit. Prior experience in the area is also attractive to funding agencies. I met many such ex-volunteers turned students in Togo, Niger and Burkina Faso, some of them geographers, and in many instances their prior experience significantly improved the quality of their research work.

It is not impossible to hook up with missionary organisations in the field (see Nuala Gormley's contribution to this volume), although personally I believe this could exacerbate the ethical problems of one's presence in the developing world just as much as work with a large development organisation might do. Although missionary organisations may have once been invited to undertake evangelising missions in the host country, their continued presence can be extremely hard to justify (except to themselves). Although missionaries in rural areas are often extremely knowledgeable and are kind and generous hosts, anthropologists and fieldworkers rarely share their aims or motives and can be hostile to them (van der Geest & Kirby 1992). While I have seen plenty of evangelist activity potentially damaging to local culture (in Ouagadougou, for example, there is an office of American Ph.D. linguists whose sole purpose is to translate the Bible into obscure local dialects), it is true that many spiritually informed NGOs run strong environment-, or health-based, programmes in West Africa and elsewhere, and links to these may be more fruitful. One American geographer I know conducted Ph.D. fieldwork in southern Burkina Faso based at a humanitarian missionary outpost, where he enjoyed good treatment. However he remained financially independent from the organisation, had prior research permission papers, and bought his own transport.

It is also possible simply to spend time with volunteers and learn from their experience. Fieldworkers with organisations such as UNAIS (U.K.), DED (Germany), SNV (Holland), Peace Corps (U.S.A.), VED (pan-European), VSO (U.K.) and AFVP (France) have an established presence in some intimidating corners of the world, and their volunteers can be particularly good 'tour guides', friends, or even informants in their own right. To some extent, they provide an alternative community to office-bound bureaucrats, intellectuals and academics, and are exactly the sort of people most practically minded students instantly identify with. Many of them were, or will be, students (see above), and understand the research process. Most enjoy few luxuries, have low spending power, are based in rural areas and are in touch with the pulse of local life - despite their 'outsider' status. Only a few continental European volunteers are sufficiently well paid to afford expensive creature comforts. As fellow outsiders, volunteers can help in understanding local culture. Most have considerable latitude from their sponsoring agency, enjoy company in their sometimes lonely outposts, and are frequently able to offer temporary accommodation as well as lifts, introductions and conversation. Volunteers should never be dismissed as a lowly class of development workers who get sick a lot and are simply in it for the thrill and the 'experience'. In northern Burkina Faso, German and French volunteers have been deeply implicated in the struggle to redress food security issues and falling soil fertility since the 1970s, and have been instrumental in developing sustainable and locally appropriate methods of land protection, and soil and water conservation.

Teaming Up

One of the most frustrating aspects of conducting cross-cultural fieldwork is the feeling that, as an outsider, a rich set of meanings and nuance remain permanently obscured by the social distance between self and other. Malinowski (1967) vented his frustration at his own difficulties of comprehension, taking this further to pass judgement on his hosts' culture and social practices. For first-time researchers in particular, being the only white face, or only westerner, is disconcerting and can lead to questioning one's purpose in doing research at all when one appears so ignorant of local cultural symbols and custom and is obviously treated with suspicion. The academic researcher seems to stand alone, culturally isolated, attempting to valorise a research proposal written months ago in a research library (Deveraux & Hoddinott 1992, 15).

A rarely mentioned mechanism to tackle this isolation and break down barriers is to work in tandem with a student(s) from the host country, conducting parallel research in the same geographical area, or collaborating on certain research topics.[3] This is particularly appropriate in areas where fewer formal organisations, such as NGOs, exist. It is always

---

[3] See Georgina Endfield and Peter O'Connor's chapter for a discussion of team work in physical geography.

worth making direct contact with students at the local university (if there is one), as well as introducing oneself to the academic staff there; they may be able to suggest current, or up-coming, student projects. In much of Africa, students must undertake extensive fieldwork themselves as part of their higher degrees in rural development, or geography - we are not the only ones engaged in this odd exercise. Many face a considerable struggle to raise the necessary funds to do so, yet may have profound knowledge that they are happy to share in exchange for access to new ideas and literature, or accommodation and transport that they could not otherwise afford. It may be appropriate to publicise their work outside the country, or to introduce them to new contacts in one's own circles. I have always felt that mutually productive work with fellow students is a very satisfactory way to bridge social distance, but also to 'give back' in a different way, and above all to learn. Differences of race and affluence never go away but can be minimised by open communication and sensitivity. In the project in which I worked, several Burkinabè researchers engaged on masters programmes worked alongside a very small number of Europeans. Their work rates, field stamina and quality of presentations certainly put my own performance in the shade, and yet they had far less financial support and backup. The results of these studies have been impressive.

Opportunistic Contacts and Encounters

Stepping back from the terrain of formal 'affiliations', it is vital to recognise that in everyday life people rarely manage to follow plans to the letter, and that some of the best research begins opportunistically, through curiosity and a desire to discover (Buttimer 1993). Delamont refers to this as 'opportunity sampling', or, more descriptively, 'snowballing' (Delamont 1992, 70, see also Rabinow's work in Morocco, 1977). Snowballing involves seizing the chance offered by a setting, or a respondent, when the opportunity presents itself, and unfolding a programme of investigation from sequential, or overlapping, chance encounters over a longer time period. Again, such approaches are pursued by chance, or by necessity, by many postgraduate students, whose fieldwork has begun from simple observation and dwelling in a location. They are equally common in anthropology, where a series of chance encounters may be used to triangulate, or deepen, understanding of a particular symbolic practice or custom. Alison Spedding's doctoral work on coca production in Bolivia first involved tentative contacts with coca producers in remote areas, which later 'snowballed' into detailed ethnographic work after long periods of confidence-building (Times Higher 1994). She had almost no contact with academic institutions over this time since the delicate question of local acceptance demanded few outside links as well as the adoption of local custom and living styles. While chaotic events and chance meetings pervade most if not all fieldwork experiences of this sort, making the most of them may require some persistence.

Conclusions

Several conclusions pertain from the remarks made here on different affiliation strategies. Firstly, mutually profitable institutional affiliations are often the hardest to discover and to maintain during fieldwork. Effort and persistence, however, often pay off; and some of the cases above demonstrate that even the more unpromising options open to students (those where real academic constraints might exist in projects or big international organisations) can be turned around to allow for sensitive research which crosses cultural divides and maintains ethical responsibility. Doing things differently in any 'alternative' way may involve some personal costs, financial outlay, the sacrifice of time, or security. Yet at the heart of my own predilection for doing fieldwork differently and searching out alternative ways to get doctoral work done, is a concern recently voiced by Kim England who suggests 'potentially exploitative' relationships with the 'researched' are all too common and hard to avoid (England 1994, 82). As privileged outsiders, western ethnographers and geographers can find the misuse of one's position difficult to check and exploitative situations are always hard to identify and control. Inventiveness over research practice may keep one on one's toes in this regard.

Secondly, I offer a practical strategy as advice. A good plan, upon arrival in the country, is to approach the more conventional institutions (universities may be included here) if they exist, but also to *seek out* those organisations most active in the field, most in touch with the issues you wish to address, and most in accord with your *own* ideals and values. This does not mean that caution be thrown to the winds, the requirements of funding bodies be avoided, or that national research clearances be circumvented. It does suggest a degree of experimentation and openness, and perhaps a bit of faith too. Organisations and individuals not in accordance with your own beliefs, but nonetheless influential, also need to be spoken to. Copies of all research output need to make their way back to university departments and libraries, or to projects and local people, to act as reference sources.

Thirdly, questions of financing always loom large. A measure of financial independence may lead to greater acceptance in some organisations, particularly in poorly funded NGOs, or grassroots groups. This cannot be denied, and yet other organisations, particularly those with international donor sources behind them, may be in a position to offer basic support. Good fieldwork can be done cheaply if backed up locally, and it is always possible to re-apply for funding once installed; an arranged affiliation may strengthen future funding applications.

Fourthly, not all visitors to remote areas arrive at opportune moments; not all projects or agencies are welcoming. Yet my own experience is that visitors are rarely turned away, even if they may be asked to wait for pressures of work to subside a little. Development projects, like farms, are seasonal things; certain periods are more stressful than others. Honesty about ones' motivation and aims usually goes further than anything else to allay suspicion in non-academic environments; this also applies to setting up affiliations, not just interviewing and writing up (Hammersley & Atkinson 1983, 83). Organisations are unlikely to be impressed by the facility with which you concealed your true motives in discussions with them, even if this may seem a good 'way in' at the time.

PASSING THROUGH - Fieldwork isn't Everything
The tenor of these reflections has been to suggest a broader conception of fieldwork politics and agendas than is often acknowledged by geographers. Learning in part from current postgraduate research projects I use these experiences to suggest alternative affiliations, or positions, from which research may be conducted. Hopefully my own position on overseas work involving applied elements is clear. My belief is that geographers involved in field research are ideally placed to act on the interface between local people and external (possibly international) institutions, agencies, or projects. Since the latter are increasingly implicated in local livelihood systems, researchers can act as 'conduits', or 'brokers', transmitting 'ideas and resources' in both directions (Bebbington 1993, 174) and can interpret actor rationales at the same time (Long 1992). This approach recognises the essential 'difference' of the researcher from his/her hosts, the partiality of his/her perspective, and acknowledges one is "... neither an insider nor an outsider in any absolute sense, but rather an interlocutor." (Nast 1994, 60). From such a conceptual position, personal politics can be played out on the borders of the self, the locality, and the institutions active within it. If this positioning is at all supportable - and not everybody believes it to be so - two propositions follow from it.

Firstly, under this rubric of working on the 'interface', emancipatory research (that which is not self-serving) must become less the terrain of those once perceived as idealists and radicals and enter mainstream geography as an accepted, sound and sympathetic way to bridge divides and encourage the community to 'do something' (Knight, 1986) and to question its persistent Euro-Americanist discourse (Slater 1992, 308). Even today, peripheral regions and their people remain absent from the vast majority of geographical work, and applied research rarely receives the recognition and support it deserves. Kim England poses a further question: whether, given "the inevitability of unequal power relations in fieldwork, we should even be doing this research at all" (England 1994, 86)? Like her, I am equivocal. A partial response in the case of overseas fieldwork in developing areas is to say that the particular asymmetry of power relations that can so easily emerge can and must be acknowledged and then *channelled* in order to make one's personal geography relevant. Channelling involves more than extricating data for a dissertation, or a paper (a process which Robert Chambers (1983) calls 'data mining'), or pursuing pure ethnographies as an 'escape' from one's own culture (e.g. Rabinow 1977). Frankly, for all my own questionnaires and surveys, I obtained most personal satisfaction lobbying local NGOs for the provision of basic services, and assisting farmers in the construction of rudimentary soil protection works. While this may sound rather haughty, it is unfortunate that some funding bodies and supervisors deem such activities to be off the point, or deride the possibility of geographical advocacy - such things have never been popular (Bebbington & Carney 1990, di Leonardo 1989).

Secondly, and to return again to Geertz and Long's actor perspective, situating oneself as an intermediary between local groups and the wider community is simply a good way to get research done in its own right: research *can* be done this way. Acting as a 'broker' between actors and institutions facilitates broad-based and satisfying interpretations of social phenomena which trace causality and local nuance. Pragmatically, the intermediary role can help justify one's uneasy presence in a place no-one expects you to be, since maintaining affiliations or links with institutions assists the breakdown of cultural difference. The key point here is that the *conditions* under which the actual fieldwork leading to scholarly output is conducted are equally important as (and affect) the *carrying out* of that research. Situating oneself, through a well thought-out affiliation, can aid in the collection and interpretation of primary data and its subsequent elaboration in conceptual, comparative or theoretical work. In fact, it is helpful to consider the affiliation question as proposed here alongside the call by Turner (1989) for a 'specialist-synthesist merger' in geographical inquiry. His 'merger' argument and agenda recognises the need to make direct investigations in defined areas and to relate these to complex webs of variables and processes acted out on a wider geographical tapestry. Geographers involved in intermediary positions within organisations are, I contend, well placed to make these sorts of links and connections.

I would like to conclude in a challenging way, by presenting two alternative images which have less to say about affiliations and intermediary roles in research, and more about human strengths and weaknesses. I introduce them here simply to remind all of us that overseas fieldwork involves special qualities of fortitude and courage, and that these should not be glossed over either. These personal qualities also constitute part of the structural conditions underlying the fieldwork experience.

To what extent Malinowski's diaries may have shaken up the anthropology community over the last twenty-five years is difficult to assess. The exposure of his true self, his own state of mind and reservations over alien cultures truly teaches an important lesson. Despite his personal shortcomings, his method was such that the research was done. This story made me realise that fieldwork demands not just skills and good 'positioning' through local alliances, but also an element of courage. This was brought home at a meeting of the Royal Geographical Society (31 Jan. 1994) which provides the first concluding image. Amidst the pomposity of the Chair's remarks and the rustle of unweathered Barbours in the audience, Ffyona Campbell, whose own failings, like Malinowski, have been published recently, talked of the explorations of her own spirit, and of the African continent, which she walked from end to end. She talked of her ability to 'suspend' sensory perception and enter 'into daydreams' while covering huge distances on foot and negotiating daily torments including sickness, injury and seemingly hopeless periods of waiting. Seeing through and completing a different sort of 'grand project' like this, in these post-colonial times - even if not carried out with humanitarian aims at heart - says volumes about personal commitment and psychological strength. This is not a cliché. Capturing an other-worldly geographical imagination not by wordy prose, but by accomplishment, says more to me about the latent possibilities of the human spirit (Buttimer 1993) and its ability to carve out hope from a pervasive vision of African diversity, struggle, crisis and despair than I, supposedly a 'geographical fieldworker', could ever do.

The second image pursues this issue of courage and accomplishment down a different and equally treacherous path. While I had read Drèze and Sen's major work on Hunger and Public Action (1990) with approval and knew of Sen's great recognition, I was ignorant of Jean Drèze's personal altruism and how this related to his work. This was reported in a short article which was published as Drèze was preparing peaceful protests against the Gulf War on the Iraq-Kuwait border (Pilkington 1990). Drèze's courage, drawn in part of religious commitment and a burning sense of injustice, has taken a different course to Campbell's. During doctoral work in New Delhi in the early 1980s he tried to break down a perceived social distance with the slum dwellers of his study and moved in with them, later donating his entire student grant to charity and living a penniless existence. He has chosen an austere, homeless life ever since, and resigned his academic post in London. In his words,

> "...I believe that we have to be involved in the world to write about it. I use my research as one way of expressing my concern for the world, just as I use peace action......I know it will take years for the world to improve, but I believe we can start making changes on a personal level here and now. We must practice what we preach...."
>
> (Drèze quoted in Pilkington 1990).

His philosophy of total involvement and equality with the researched inspires guilt, puzzlement and admiration, as his interviewer points out. How many could live out their own beliefs in this way, or emulate his actions, no matter how strongly they maintain them?

While this argument has been about ameliorating the conditions under which our own 'fieldwork' may prosper, and affiliations are central to this, it must never be forgotten that we circulate in privileged worlds shackled to the need to 'discover', to get our data, and to perhaps enjoy fleeting recognition. Perhaps what is needed is not just rich and revealing research methodologies (cf. Geertz 1983) - supported by fruitful affiliations with organisations relevant to the research project and to local concerns - but also something more, an element of courage that must come from within *us*, as these two examples hint at. Not all of us practice what we preach, least of all in foreign countries. Others outside the postgraduate lounge and the coffee room already occupy a terrain of inner strength, solitude and sometimes visionary fortitude. For me, they are the real geographers.

GLOSSARY
(Names of organisations are given in English, not the original language)

ACORD	Agency for Co-operation in Research and Development
AFVP	Association of French volunteers
APAD	Euro-African Association for the Anthropology of Social Change and Development
CGIAR	Consultative Group on International Agricultural Research
CIP	International Potato Center
CIAT	Center for Tropical Agricultural Research
DED	German development volunteers

ESRC   Economic and Social Research Council
GTZ   German technical assistance organisation
IRRI   International Rice Research Institute
ICRISAT   International Crops Research Institute for the Semi-Arid
            Tropics
IIED   International Institute for Environment and Development
ODA   Overseas Development Administration
ORSTOM   French institute for scientific research and
            development co-operation
OXFAM   Oxford Committee for Famine Relief
PAF   Oxfam Agro-Forestry Project, Yatenga, Burkina Faso
PATECORE   Project for land management and natural resource
            conservation
            on the Central Plateau Burkina Faso
NGO   Non Governmental Organisation
SNV   Netherlands volunteer service
UNAIS   United Nations Association International Service
USAID   United States Agency for International Development
VED   European volunteers for development
VSO   Voluntary Service Overseas

REFERENCES

Ayers, Alison J. 1992 'Conflicts of Complementarities? The State and NGOs in the Colonisation Zones of San Julian and Berlin, Eastern Bolivia' Agricultural Administration (Research & Extension) Network Paper 37 London: Overseas Development Institute.

Barnes, Trevor J. & Duncan, James S. (eds) 1992 Writing Worlds, Discourse, Text and Metaphor in the Representation of Landscape London: Routledge.

Batterbury, Simon 1996 Planners or Performers? Reflections on Indigenous Dryland Farming in Northern Burkina Faso Agriculture and Human Values 13, 3, 12-22.

Bebbington, Anthony J. 1990 Indigenous Agriculture in the Central Ecuadorian Andes, the Cultural Ecology and Institutional Conditions of its Construction and its Change Ph.D. dissertation Worcester MA: Graduate School of Geography, Clark University.

Bebbington, Anthony J. 1993 'Peasant federations, development institutions, and technological change in the Andes' in Glade, William & Reilly, Charles A. (eds) Inquiry at the Grassroots, an Inter-American Foundation Fellowship Reader Washington D.C: Inter-American Foundation, 153-176.

Bebbington, Anthony J. & Carney, Judy 1990 'Geographers in the international agricultural research centers, theoretical and practical considerations' Annals of the Association of American Geographers 80, 1, 34-48.

Bebbington, Anthony J. & Thiele, Graham 1993 <u>Non-Governmental Organisations and the State in Latin America, Rethinking Roles in Sustainable Agricultural Development</u> London: Routledge.

Breheny, Michael J. 1989 'Chalkface to Coalface, a review of the academic-practice interface' <u>Environment & Planning B, Planning & Design</u> 16, 451-468.

Buttimer, Anne 1993 <u>Geography and the Human Spirit</u> Baltimore: Johns Hopkins University Press.

Byron, Margaret 1993 'Using audio-visual aids in geography: Questions of access and responsibility' <u>Area</u> 25, 4, 379-385.

Chambers, Robert 1983 <u>Rural Development: Putting the Last First</u> Harlow: Longman.

Chambers, Robert 1993 <u>Challenging the Professions, Frontiers for Rural Development</u> London: Intermediate Technology.

Clark, John 1991 <u>Democratising Development: The Role of Voluntary Organisations</u> London: Earthscan.

Clifford, James 1986 'Introduction, Partial Truths' in Clifford, James & Marcus, George (eds) <u>Writing Culture, the Poetics and Politics of Ethnography</u> Berkeley: University of California Press, 1-27.

Clifford, James & Marcus, George E. (eds) 1986 <u>Writing Culture, the Poetics and Politics of Ethnography</u> Berkeley: University of California Press.

Delamont, Sara 1992 <u>Fieldwork in Educational Settings, Methods, Pitfalls and Perspectives</u> London: Falmer Press.

Deveraux, Stephen & Hoddinott, John 1992 'The Context of Fieldwork' in Deveraux, S. & Hoddinott, J. (eds) <u>Fieldwork in Developing Countries</u> London: Harvester Wheatsheaf, 3-24.

Drèze, Jean & Sen, Amartya 1989 <u>Hunger and Public Action</u> Oxford: Oxford University Press.

Dumont, René 1986 <u>Pour l'Afrique, j'accuse. Le journal d'un agronome au Sahel en voie de destruction</u> Collection Terre Humaine, Paris: Librairie Plon/Presses Pocket.

England, Kim V.L. 1994. 'Getting personal: Reflexivity, positionality, and feminist research' <u>Professional Geographer</u> 46, 1, 80-89.

Fairhead, James 1993 'Representing knowledge, the 'New Farmer' in research fashions' in Pottier, Johan (ed) <u>Practising Development, Social Science Perspectives</u> London: Routledge, 187-204.

Francis, Elizabeth 1992 'Qualitative research, collecting life histories' in Deveraux, Stephen & Hoddinott, John (eds) Fieldwork in Developing Countries London: Harvester Wheatsheaf, 86-101.

Friedmann, John 1992 Empowerment: the Politics of Alternative Development Oxford: Blackwell.

Geertz, Clifford 1983 (orig. pub. 1974 Bulletin of the American Academy of Arts and Sciences 28, 1) 'From the native's point of view: On the nature of anthropological understanding' in Geertz, C. (ed) Local Knowledge, Further Essays in Interpretive Anthropology New York: Basic Books, 55-70.

van der Geest, Sjaak & Kirby, Jon P. 1992 'The absence of the missionary in African ethnography 1930-65' African Studies Review 35, 3, 59-103.

Goffman, Erving 1959 The Presentation of Self in Everyday Life New York: Doubleday Anchor Books.

Gubbels, Peter 1992 Farmer-First Research, Populist Pipedream or Practical Paradigm, Prospects for Indigenous Agricultural Self-Development in West Africa M.A. dissertation (Development Studies), University of East Anglia.

Gubbels, Peter 1993 'Peasant farmer organisation in farmer-first agricultural development in West Africa, new opportunities and continuing constraints' Agricultural Administration (Research & Extension) Network Paper 40 London: Overseas Development Institute.

Hammersley, Martyn & Atkinson, Paul 1983 Ethnography: Principles in Practice London: Routledge.

Hooper, Jonathan 1989 The Effect of Farmer-Built Filtrating Dike Systems on Increasing Soil Fertility and Reversing Soil Degradation in the Sahelo-Sudanian Zone of West Africa M.Sc. thesis (Soil Science), North Carolina State University.

IIED/PATECORE 1993 La pertinence de la methode accelerée de recherche participative dans la gestion des terroirs villageois, rapport final de l'atelier sur le MARP organisé par PATECORE de 15-25 Octobre 1992 Kongoussi, Burkina Faso, Projet d'Aménagement de Terroirs et Conservation des Ressources au Plateau Central; London: International Institute for Environment & Development.

Katz, Cindi 1994 'Playing the field: Questions of fieldwork in ethnography' Professional Geographer 46, 1, 67-72.

Knight, Peter 1986 'Why doesn't Geography do something?' Area 18, 4, 333-334.

di Leonardo, M. 1989 'Malinowski's Nephews' The Nation 13 March, 350-352.

Lindskog, Per & Mando, Abdoulaye 1992 'The Relationship Between Research Institutes and NGOs in the Field of Soil and Water Conservation in Burkina Faso' Dryland Networks Programme Issue Paper 39 London: International Institute for Environment & Development.

Long, Norman 1992 'From paradigm lost to paradigm regained? The case for an actor-oriented sociology of development' in Long, Norman & Long, Anne (eds) Battlefields of Knowledge, the Interlocking of Theory & Practice in Social Development London: Routledge, 16-43.

van Maanen, Jon 1988 Tales of the Field, On Writing Ethnography Chicago: University of Chicago Press.

Madge, Clare 1993 'Boundary disputes, comments on Sidaway (1992)' Area 25, 3, 294-299.

Malinowski, Bronislaw 1967 A Diary in the Strict Sense of the Term New York: Harcourt Brace & World.

Mercer, David 1984 'Unmasking technocratic geography' in Billinge, Mark, Gregory, Derek & Martin, Ron (eds) Recollections of a Revolution: Geography as Spatial Science Critical Human Geography Series. London: Macmillan, 153-199.

Mills, Charles Wright 1959 The Sociological Imagination New York: Oxford University Press.

Nast, Heidi J. 1994 'Opening Remarks on "Women in the Field"' Professional Geographer 46, 1, 54-66.

Ndione, Emmanuel, Philippe de Leener, Mamadou Ndiaye, Pierre Jacolin, Jean-Pierre Perier. 1995. The Future of Community Lands: Human Resources. London: Intermediate Technology. [Reviewed in Local Environment, 1(2) 238-240, by Simon Batterbury]

Peil, Margaret 1982 Social Science Research Methods: An African Perspective Sevenoaks: Hodder & Stoughton.

Pilkington, Edward 1990 'Down and Out by Preference' The Independent 15 November p20.

Potter, Rob 1993 'Little England and Little Geography, reflections on Third World teaching and research' Area 25, 3, 291-294.

Rabinow, Paul 1977 Reflections on Fieldwork in Morocco Berkeley: University of California Press.

Razavi, Shahrashoub 1992 'Fieldwork in a familiar setting, the role of politics at the national, community and household levels' in Deveraux, Stephen & Hoddinott, John (eds) Fieldwork in Developing Countries London: Harvester Wheatsheaf, 152-163.

Roche, Chris 1984 'Cereal banks in Burkina Faso - a case study' Liverpool Papers in Human Geography 18 Department of Geography, Liverpool University.

Rogers, Ali 1991 'The boundaries of reason, social and cultural geography and the world' in Philo, Chris (compiler) New Words, New Worlds, Reconceptualising Social and Cultural Geography Lampeter: St David's University College, 131-143.

Sidaway, James D. 1992 'In other worlds: on the politics of 'first world' geographers in the 'third world'' Area 24, 403-408.

Slater, David 1992 'On the borders of social theory, learning from other regions' Environment & Planning D, Society & Space 10, 307-327.

Times Higher 1994 'Coca Harvest Reaps Research Bonus' Times Higher 15 April, p7.

Torres, Gabriel 1992 'Plunging into the garlic: methodological issues and challenges' in Long, Norman & Long, Anne (eds) Battlefields of Knowledge: the Interlocking of Theory & Practice in Social Development London: Routledge, 85-114.

Toulmin, Camilla 1992 Cattle, Women & Wells: Managing Household Survival in the Sahel Oxford: Clarendon.

Turner, Billie Lee II 1989 'The specialist-synthesis approach to the revival of geography: the case of cultural ecology' Annals of the Association of American Geographers 79, 1, 88-100.

Wilson, Ken 1992 'Thinking about the ethics of fieldwork' in Deveraux, Stephen & Hoddinott, John (eds) Fieldwork in Developing Countries London: Harvester Wheatsheaf, 179-199.

7.

THE ETHICS OF RESEARCH IN THE 'THIRD WORLD'
Clare Madge

INTRODUCTION[1]
This chapter considers some of the ethical issues involved in undertaking research in the 'Third World'.[2] I have decided that the most effective way to produce a short discussion on such an important, emotive and huge topic is to distil my thoughts into a few key questions that I consider to be of relevance to postgraduates about to 'embark' on research in the Third World. The chapter also speaks to the wider audience of established researchers, and many of the questions raised are also pertinent for those undertaking research in a First World context. Moreover, although the chapter focuses on research carried out in the Third World by people from the First World, some of the issues will be similar (and others different) for Third World researchers investigating both the First and Third Worlds.[3]

The aim of the chapter is not to provide any 'neat' answers, but to stimulate discussion and debate about a topic that I feel has not had a great 'airing' in the published geographical literature (although it has been deliberated at length both in the 'private' sphere of geography's academic circles and in the published 'development' literature, e.g. Crocker 1991,

---

[1] I am very grateful to two anonymous referees for their insightful comments on this chapter.

[2] Throughout this chapter the term 'Third World' is employed to refer to those nations which, during the process of the formation of the existing world order, did not become materially rich due to their peripherality in a system produced by the expansion of world capital. The diversity of cultures, economies and political strategies within this group of countries is acknowledged. 'First World' is employed to denote societies which became 'developed' through the 'underdevelopment' of Africa, Asia, Latin America and the Caribbean. However, reservation is expressed about the use of the term, owing to the diversity of countries, societies and values within the First and Third Worlds and their changing political and economic positioning on a global scale. Furthermore, the concept is a 'figment of the imagination' which embodies imperialistic assumptions and, through its focus on spatially-fixed boundaries and territorial divisions, is divisive for the creation of potential alliances and oppositional struggles to the lines of power (Mohanty 1991). However, the term is used (with reservation) in this chapter 'as the worst term, apart from all the others'.

[3] See the chapter by Uwem Ite for a more detailed discussion of the particular issues associated with doing research 'at home'.

Goulet 1990, Gunatilleke et al. 1983, Sen 1987). The chapter is based on my relatively limited research experience of Ph.D. investigations in one village in The Gambia, West Africa and the subsequent four years of reflection after having been 'there'.

QUESTION 1: WHAT DOES ETHICAL RESEARCH MEAN?

Before embarking on any discussion of the ethics of research in the Third World it is first necessary to explore the term 'ethical research'. What exactly does it mean? After investigating the literature (Burgess 1984, Cassell and Wax 1980, Hall 1982, Homan 1991, Seiber 1992, Wilson 1992), it appears that ethical research is commonly understood to be research that 'does no harm', which gains informed consent from, and respects the rights of, the individuals being studied. I find this understanding of the term problematic for several reasons.

First, if this concept 'to do no harm' was followed rigidly, then it would paralyse most researchers for, as Patai (1991, 137) notes, rarely can we measure, let alone determine, the potential consequences of our research.

Second, gaining informed consent from the research population to ensure that they genuinely understand the purpose of the research, the source of funding and how the results might be used, is not a simple issue. Such an understanding of the research will be subject to interpretation from within the cultural framework of the research population and will change with time. Moreover, consent also invariably involves some form of reciprocal arrangement, whereby the researcher also 'gives something back' to the community (Scheper-Hughes 1992, 18).

Third, (ideally, theoretically), I believe that ethical research should not only 'do no harm', but also have potential 'to do good', to involve 'empowerment' (and I use the term with reservation) of the people with whom one works, to involve some form of empowering social transformation (although the extent to which this is possible is open to debate, especially if the researcher solely plays the role of academic).

Fourth, one cannot, therefore, assume that the interpretation of the meaning of ethical research is universal. This is inevitable, for ethics is a philosophy of morality, and moral judgements are obviously evaluative and subjective. What is ethical research to me as a person from England, might not be ethical to a person from The Gambia. Determinations of what ethical research means will depend on 'positionality'; on our class, nationality, sexuality, race, gender, religion. It will also, as academics, depend on the stage in our career and on our position in academia and the world beyond.

Fifth, the ethics of research in practice does not refer to abstract 'correct' behaviour, or a neat consent form to be filled in, but to a living relationship between the person doing the research and the people who are the subject of that research. This relationship is not fixed but changes through time. Consequently, different ethical issues are at stake at different points in the research process. For example, the ethical issues arising during the data collection process (e.g. do I 'compensate' my informants for their time and information?) are different from those arising during the writing and/or publishing process (e.g. do I send the informants a copy of my thesis even though they may dislike/disagree with my analysis?). Furthermore, the research relationship upon which ethical research rests not only varies in time, but it also varies with place; it has a geographical dimension. The ethics of research will depend on the structural relationships between the countries involved. For example, the ethical issues raised during my research would have been very different if I had undertaken my research in Mexico rather than in The Gambia, or if I had come from Mauritius rather than England.

So, in trying to answer the question 'What does ethical research mean?', I would suggest that it means different things to different people, and that its meaning alters with time and place: ethical research does not have a universally understood meaning. Specifically, you might like to think about what your ethical 'positioning' is before going to do your research in the Third World, and try to anticipate some of the ethical issues that might arise at various points during your fieldwork.

QUESTION 2: IS ETHICAL RESEARCH POSSIBLE (IN AN UNETHICAL WORLD)? (PATAI 1991)

According to Patai (1991) the brief answer is 'no'.[4] She suggests ethical research by US academics on Third World women is not possible because we live in an unethical world. In the case of my research in The Gambia, there were times when I also felt that my research was not ethical. This was owing (amongst other things) to the political and economic global power relations between The Gambia and England which meant that research, that at minimum 'did no harm', and that potentially 'did some good', was difficult to achieve between unequally-positioned individuals and countries. It was, after all, only through the existence of 'privilege', through the existing status quo of global power relations, that I went to a Gambian village to do my research, rather than someone from that village coming to England to investigate my 'lifeworld'. I would argue, therefore,

---

[4] Patai's argument is far more substantial than this blunt assertion, but there is not space here to elaborate.

that if we want to examine the ethics of research in the Third World in any meaningful way, then we cannot ignore the global political economy of power relations, because First World researchers doing research in the Third World is not 'neutral'; it is an outcome of historical processes of inequality.

Fabian (1983, 149) suggests that he "...cannot exclude the possibility...that repetitive enactment of field research by thousands of aspiring established practitioners of anthropology has been part of a sustained effort to maintain a certain type of relationship between the West and its other." I would suggest that the same can be argued for practitioners of geography. Academic geographers are part of a system of knowledge production that has systematically undermined and dislodged Third World thought systems (ways of understanding and being) and created powerful institutions of knowledge which are located in the First World, and often (but not always) viewed from the perspective of the First World.[5] As academics, we are situated within this unequal political economy and can (unwittingly) produce 'stories' and perspectives that are aligned to such centres of power and privilege. Such power of knowledge has been termed 'academic imperialism' by Ake (1979).

This second question is therefore interesting, for when we start to consider whether ethical research is possible in an unethical world, we begin to see how this thing called 'ethics' is linked to the thing called 'power' and also to the production of knowledge itself. Often ethics is simply equated with personal politics; I would also argue that it is linked to global politics. The academy plays an important role in upholding (and, sometimes, subverting) that global dynamic. Who, for example, defines the meaning of ethical research in books, dictionaries and for grant-awarding bodies? It strikes me that perhaps the minimum requirement of ethical research being research that 'does no harm' may be a way in which the unequal relations between the First and Third Worlds are perpetuated and remain unchallenged. Is it a means of (un)consciously perpetuating who has the right (or opportunity) to speak, a means of selectively filtering who is creating knowledge about the Third World and in what terms and in which language? (see Ngugi Wa Thiong'o 1992). What would the academy look like (and be like) if ethical research was commonly understood to be research which 'did good', which led to empowering social transformation?

So a second question aspiring postgraduates might like to ask is, 'Given your definition of ethics, is ethical research possible (indeed

---

[5] I am not suggesting that all forms of 'Western' knowledge are disempowering in a Third World context (see Nanda 1991), but Hobart (1993), Long & Long (1992) and Warren (1989) have documented case studies illustrating the destruction of 'indigenous' knowledge through contact with 'Western' knowledge systems.

desirable) in your research project, in the context of existing global political and economic power relations?'

QUESTION 3: HOW ARE ETHICS, POWER AND KNOWLEDGE INTERCONNECTED?

In the previous section I suggested that ethics, power and knowledge are interconnected. I now want to illustrate concretely, in lived examples, how this is so. I shall argue that if we wish to explore the ethics of research in the Third World, we must also attempt to understand the power relations involved in the research process. This is clearly a very complex task because this thing called 'power' operates at a variety of scales, is relational and is exercised from numerous 'points'. As I have indicated previously, there is a global political economy of power relations in which First World academics have been able to produce knowledge about Third World people in a relatively one-way flow of information, and in which the right to write is often assumed, or not discussed, in the public arena of the geographic discipline.

However, there are other levels at which power relations operate and I now wish to focus on inter-personal power relations, for most research is based on some degree of relationship with other human beings and every human relationship inevitably involves some degree of power relation. Moreover, the only way that I have found it possible to make some sense of the enormously complex issue of ethics, knowledge and power has been by starting with myself and considering my role in the research process and by working 'outwards' from there. Below I briefly consider two examples of inter-personal power relations that operated during my fieldwork in The Gambia and demonstrate how these relationships were intimately linked to ethical issues and the production of knowledge.

Example 1: My research in The Gambia employed a plurality of research methods, but participant observation played an important role. A prominent aspect of participatory research is the idea that the researcher can maintain a "delicate balance of distance and closeness" (Shaffir & Stebbins 1991, 143), being at the same time an 'insider' and an 'outsider'. Advocates of participatory research suggest that we should become involved in the 'lifeworld' of the research population, build up personal relationships, become friends. Yet the analysis, writing up and dissemination of information often forces us to detach ourselves, switch back to 'Western mode' to produce texts and develop 'distance' to use information gained through friendships. In other words, to become a stranger. In reality, I found this delicate balance laden with complications. How can one be both a friend and a stranger? Indeed, as Jarvie (1982, 68) suggests, to play the roles of friend and stranger with integrity, while trying to combine them is impossible (see also Facio 1993, Rose 1993).[6] An example will best illustrate this point.

During my year's stay in The Gambia I learnt much 'privileged information' through my personal relationships with individuals, informally chatting or by participation in day-to-day activities. However, after becoming a friend, I did not feel that I could suddenly become the detached stranger on my return to England and use such information for my academic advancement.[7] For example, I learnt much privileged information about the use of herbal medicines for 'women's' complaints, but although an integral aspect of my study was the role that herbal medicines played in rural Gambia, I did not use the information about women's herbal medicines in my thesis. To do so would have been to betray the trust of my friends, and, as in this context knowledge is linked to power, I may also have disempowered them through the use of such information (I was sending the villagers a copy of my thesis so anyone could have gained access to that specialised 'secret' medicinal knowledge).[8]

This example renders suspect the validity of the dichotomous divisions of friend and stranger. Rather, I suggest that participant observation involves playing out a multiplicity of changing roles during the course of the research. These roles, which are sometimes complementary, sometimes clashing, and which are contingent on our positionality, will influence the data given/gained and our subsequent interpretations. In other words, they will influence what we produce as knowledge. Personal relationships with people will influence the ethical decisions we make regarding what we create as knowledge. Power, ethics and knowledge are interconnected.

Example 2: When I first started living in the village, I insisted on washing my own clothes because the thought of anyone else doing my

---

6 Comaroff & Comaroff (1992, 27) ask whether a "sense of hope and despair" is intrinsic to ethnography. They suggest that its relativism bequeaths to it an "enduring sense of its own limitations, its own irony". Perhaps, then, the 'delicate balance' is an inevitable outcome of the ethnographic method?

7This situation is, I am certain, common. Most researchers face the dilemma of whether or not to use certain information gained in the field. I am not, therefore, arguing that my actions here were more honourable than other academics. What I am attempting to illustrate is the connection between ethical positioning and knowledge creation.

8 'Disempowerment' refers to the process by which the power, status and position of a group is reduced at the level of inter-personal relationships and/or at the macro level. It refers to a reduced ability to challenge structures of domination and a diminished potential to create alternatives to existing structures.

domestic work for me was abhorrent; it was unethical to me. However, this insistence was insulting to the family with whom I was living, as I only understood at a later date. Any 'stranger' that visits a Gambian family is treated with 'respect' and 'hospitality' which includes not undertaking heavy domestic work - at least for the first few months of a visit. While my insistence to wash my own clothes was because I did not want to get any special 'privileges' because of my nationality and, racial and gendered identity, (being a white woman from the First World), this insistence was itself based on a privileged positioning. Rather than acknowledging my 'whiteness', the fact I was from 'there', and that I was 'rich', I wished to obscure these things, to conceal my difference, to shroud my (material) power, and to wish away the historical relations that surrounded it.[9] In other words, I tried to ignore the political economy of power relations. However, this is not possible: interpersonal relations are embedded within this political economy.

The interesting point is that when I started thinking through why I had insisted on doing my own washing, and in particular seeing how this action was linked to my self-identity as a white woman, my idea about what was ethical behaviour altered. As views about myself and my relationship with other people changed, so did my understanding of the 'lifeworld' of the people I was living with. This altered my access to and interpretation of 'data'. Indeed, it was at the moment when I no longer insisted on washing my own clothes that (retrospectively) people said that they had started to trust me and to share information previously withheld. Data collected does, therefore, depend on what informants are willing to reveal, which depends on their appraisal of, and the trust they place in, the researcher. Again, power, knowledge and ethical issues are interconnected.

I give these examples for it is through a consideration of these 'boundary disputes' (Bhabha 1983) these 'moments' of trouble and dislocation, that we can open up 'spaces' to examine how we see ourselves and our relationships with the people with whom we are living and working (Madge, 1993). Through a consideration of these spaces we can place interpersonal power politics (an academic collecting information, a woman washing clothes) within the broader political economy (a First World white female academic) and see how these are linked to understandings, interpretations and decisions regarding ethical issues. Through trying to comprehend what I was/am and what I was/am not, by

---

[9] According to Frankenberg (1993) 'whiteness' is not only a location of structural advantage, of race privilege, but it is also a place, a standpoint, from which white people look at themselves and others and at society. It usually refers to a set of cultural practices which are unmarked/unnamed. (See also hooks 1992).

interrogating my silences and my communications, I am starting to see how, in attempting to write about Africa, I am linked to a network of unequal power relations. Once identified, these power relations can be challenged. The important point is that our self-identity will influence the research that we do, the interpretations that we make, the knowledge we construct about the Third World and the outcomes of that research.

The question you might like to consider is, 'How are the decisions you make (or have made) regarding ethical issues linked to power relations (at varying levels with various people/institutions) and how are these decisions then translated into knowledge?'

QUESTION 4: IF ETHICAL RESEARCH IS NOT POSSIBLE THEN WHY CONTINUE TO DO RESEARCH IN THE THIRD WORLD?

Bronfenbrenner (1952, 453) asked some time ago whether the only safe way of not violating professional ethics was to refrain from doing research all together. When I returned from The Gambia I had much sympathy with this argument, particularly with specific reference to research in the Third World by people from the First World (and I still do some/much of the time). I thought perhaps the 'solution' was to do research at 'home', studying the society of which I am part. However, I am now aware that 'coming home' is also problematic; ethical dilemmas and tensions abound wherever research is undertaken.[10] Moreover, this 'coming home' stance is also problematic as it may result in further centring geographic discourse on the West, rather than on the 'rest', despite the increasingly complex relationships between the First and Third Worlds. Is 'getting out' then also potentially unethical? Scheper-Hughes (1992, 27) argues, for example, that, "Not to look, to touch, to engage can be a hostile act".

The ethics of research in the Third World is a highly complex set of issues. There are no easy answers. However, it does appear that many ethical problems are also inherently 'political' problems (in the broadest sense) thus requiring political solutions. Is then the key issue not whether ethical research is possible (or not) in the Third World, but rather what is 'made' of the knowledge that is produced and whose 'version' is taken as most authoritative (hooks 1989)?

Researchers can, for example, attempt to challenge, question and/or subvert some of the existing power relations between First and Third

---

[10] Although the dynamics of the research encounter and research relationships depend substantially upon the geographical location of the research, the power differentials are potentially greater and the ethical issues thus potentially more complex, in the situation of a First World researcher investigating the Third World. But see also Uwem Ite's chapter in this volume.

Worlds to, as Spivak has proposed (quoted in Young 1990, 172), "contest and inflict the more far-reaching implications of the system of which these relations form a part." Personally, I shall strive to consider the role I play, as an (albeit ambivalent) academic, in supporting and challenging (often simultaneously) unequal economic, political and cultural systems and to build up challenging, positive and creative personal relationships. I need to think about whether what I create as knowledge will be used to strengthen, or challenge existing systems of inequality and domination (by this I am not simply referring to the First/Third World dynamic, but also to gender, race, sexuality and poverty inequalities in this country, not just within the academy, but in my working practice and my world beyond the academy). Ultimately I must decide if the research is worth doing (why and to whom - using whose criteria?), be clear about the 'outcomes' of my research and then go about it in ways that are sensitive to, and challenging of, the power differentials involved.

So the last question you might like to think about is, 'Why are you doing your research in the Third World and what do you hope to 'make' of it?'

CONCLUSIONS

In this chapter I have argued that conducting ethical research in the Third World does not involve a simple, fixed set of formulae; rather it entails thinking through the <u>process</u> of working and living with people. It also (potentially) involves attempting to 'make something' of the research, so that it feeds into action and change and challenges the unequal power relations which enable the one-way flow of geographic information from the Third World to the First World. Additionally, conducting ethical research consists of being aware of (and including accounts of) the limitations of our knowledge and acknowledgement of how what we produce as knowledge is an outcome of a set of unequal power relations which operate at a variety of scales.

There are no simple answers to the issues of the ethics of research in the Third World. Indeed, I already feel that this chapter has many shortcomings. For example, is it too egocentric, centring the self at the expense of peripheralising the Gambian people I lived and worked with? Have I taken myself 'too seriously' and in doing so produced a divisive account, rather than one which builds upon resistance to asymmetrical relations of power? Does the chapter liberally side step the important question of whether the academy, and more particularly geography, can ever be the location of radical change and 'action research'? Finally, have I adequately considered how and why this chapter might be used to support the 'scientific academic factory'?

REFERENCES
Ake, Claude 1979 Social Science as Imperialism: The Theory of Political Development Ibadan: Ibadan University Press.

Bhabha, Homi 1983 'Difference, discrimination and the discourse of colonialism', in F. Barker et al. (eds) The Politics of Theory Colchester: University of Essex, 194-211.

Bronfenbrenner, Urie 1952 'Principals of professional ethics: Cornell studies in social growth', American Psychologist 7, 452-455.

Burgess, Robert G. 1984 In the Field: An Introduction to Field Research London: Allen and Unwin.

Cassell, Joan and Wax, M.L. 1980 'Editorial introduction: towards a moral science of human beings' Social Problems 27, 259-264.

Comaroff, John & Comaroff, J. 1992 Ethnography and the Historical Imagination Oxford: Westview Press.

Crocker, D.A. 1991 'Towards development ethics', World Development 19, 457-483.

Fabian, Johannes 1983 Time and Another. How Anthropology Makes its Object New York: Columbia University Press.

Facio, Elisa 1993 'Ethnography as personal experience', in John H. Stanfield & Rutledge M. Dennis (eds) Race and Ethnicity in Research Methods London: Sage, 75-91.

Frankenberg, Ruth 1993 White Women, Race Matters: The Social Construction of Whiteness London: Routledge.

Goulet, Denis 1990 'Development ethics and ecological wisdom', in Ronald J. Engel & Gibb Joan Engel (eds) Ethics of Environment and Development: Global Challenge, International Response London: Belhaven Press.

Gunatilleke, Godfrey, Ti'rucheluam, Neelan & Coomarasuamy, Radhika (eds) 1983 Ethical Dilemmas of Development in Asia Lexington: Lexington Books.

Hall, R. 1982 'The teaching of moral values in geography', Journal of Geography in Higher Education 7, 3-14.

Hobart, Mark 1993 (ed) An Anthropological Critique of Development London: Routledge.

Homan, Roger 1991 The Ethics of Social Research London: Longman.

hooks, Bell 1989 Talking Back: Thinking Feminist, Thinking Black Boston: South End Press.

hooks, Bell 1992 'Representing whiteness in the black imagination', in Lawrence Grossberg, Cary Nelson & Paula A. Treichler (eds) Cultural Studies London: Routledge, 338-346.

Jarvie, I.C. 1982 'The problem of ethical integrity in participant observation', in Robert G. Burgess (ed) Field Research London: Allen and Unwin, 68-72.

Long, Norman & Long Ann (eds) 1992 Battlefields of Knowledge: The Interlocking of Theory and Practice in Social Research and Development London: Routledge.

Madge, Clare 1993 'Boundary disputes: comments on Sidaway 1992' Area 25, 294-299.

Mohanty, Chandra Talpade 1991 'Introduction: cartographies of struggle. Third world women and the politics of feminism', in Chandra T. Mohanty, Ann Russo, and Lourdes Torres (eds) Third World Women and the Politics of Feminism Bloomington: Indiana University Press, 1-47.

Nanda, M. 1991 'Is modern science a western patriarchal myth? A critique of populist orthodoxy', South Asia Bulletin 11, 32-61.

Ngugi Wa Thiong'o 1992 Moving the Centre: The Struggle for Cultural Freedoms London: James Currey.

Patai, Daphne 1991 'US academics and Third World Women: Is ethical research possible?', in Sherna Berger Gluck and Daphne Patai (eds) Women's Words: The Feminist Practice of Oral History London: Routledge, 137-154.

Rose, Damaris 1993 'On feminism, method and methods in human geography: an idiosyncratic overview' Canadian Geographer 37, 57-60.

Scheper-Hughes, Nancy 1992 Death Without Weeping: The Violence of Everyday Life in Brazil Berkeley: University of California Press.

Seiber, Joan E. 1992 Planning Ethically Responsible Research: A Guide for Students and Research Review Bodies London: Sage.

Sen, Amartya 1987 On Ethics and Economics Oxford: Blackwells.

Shaffir, William B. and Stebbins, Robert A. (eds) 1991 Experiencing Fieldwork: An Inside View of Qualitative Research London: Sage.

Warren, D.M. 1989 'The impact of nineteenth century social science in establishing negative values and attitudes towards indigenous knowledge systems', in D.M. Warren, L.J. Slikkerveer & S.O. Titilola (eds) Indigenous Knowledge Systems: Implications for Agriculture and International Development Iowa: Iowa State University, 171-183.

Wilson, Ken 1992 'Thinking about the ethics of fieldwork', in Stephen Devereux & John Hoddinott (eds) <u>Fieldwork in Developing Countries</u> London: Harvester Wheatsheaf, 179-199.

Young, Robert 1990 <u>White Mythologies: Writing, History and the West</u> London: Routledge.

8.

LETTER FROM THE FIELD: REFLECTIONS HALF-WAY THROUGH

Nuala Bryce Gormley

Maracha Mission,
Uganda.

December 1993.

Dear Prospective Fieldworker,

I thought I would write to you to give you some thoughts about fieldwork 'from the horse's mouth'. To begin with, I should clarify that I am only half-way through my fieldwork, and so my ideas and advice on the topic could be correspondingly half-baked, but then again, there's none of the rose-coloured nostalgia of retrospect either. I offer this advice to researchers coming to conduct fieldwork in East Africa, although some of what I have to say may well be applicable in other parts of the world. As I type, tiny ants are crawling among the keys of my keyboard, and I am only able to use the computer because the local carpentry workshop has had to turn on the parish generator to mill some timber unexpectedly. If I'd known that we would only get electricity for a few hours every fortnight, I might not have bothered buying the computer, but this is just one example of 'things I wish I'd known before I came'.

I have been in Uganda for almost a year now, and will return to Edinburgh at Christmas 1994. A two year fieldwork period has both its advantages and its disadvantages. So far, I am still hoping that the former outweighs the latter. My research on the contemporary practice of mission in relation to the development of the West Nile, Uganda, is based primarily on my own personal experience as a volunteer lay-missionary in the area, necessitating a full two-year volunteer term. What I can say to you at this stage concerns practical advice, and a cautionary note about realistic objectives.

The issue of western researchers going off to 'study' non-western cultures has been heatedly debated in the history of social anthropology, and more recently in the geographical journal <u>Area</u> (Sidaway 1992, Potter 1993). In practical terms, for most geography research students, the decision to 'go' is made in the course of applying for the funding to do the research, and whether one should be going or not is not really something you spend too long thinking about.

The questions of 'Who am I when I'm there?' and 'Who will 'they' think I am?', or even "Who will I tell 'them' I am?" do occupy my thoughts, but frankly, if I spent TOO long thinking about these things, looking for an 'answer', my three year's funding would be spent at home, and nobody would be any the wiser for my efforts. With me, how I am perceived is very much a 'working concept' never far from my thoughts, but I may as well continue finding out about the things that interested me in the first place, while that issue simmers away.

I cannot stress enough that it does matter how you are perceived because it will affect your ability to carry out research and will influence the nature and quality of the information you collect. I'll offer a few examples:

RELATIVE WEALTH
At home, you may be the 'poorest' student you know, struggling from one grant payment to the next, and feeling pretty sorry for yourself. If you are conducting research in East Africa, especially in rural areas, nobody will believe that you aren't loaded. Every *Muzungu* (white person) is perceived to be wealthy. No matter how ragged your jeans, no matter how often you explain the costs of accommodation and heating in Britain, no matter how often or how convincingly you plead poverty, your local informants and friends will always think that you have access to large sums of money. In reality, compared to them, you HAVE, but still, you won't have enough to respond to even a fraction of the requests for financial aid that you will probably receive. Each case will sound valid and worthy; in fact, many requests ARE valid and worthy, but initially I suggest it is wise not to respond to requests for financial assistance. Once you have established local friends and contacts, you can sift through the genuine and bogus requests.

It would also be my advice not to spend extravagantly while in your host community - don't buy beer for the lads all night every night. It won't earn you respect, just a reputation as another *Muzungu* mug. You may well want to help out some people with school fees, funeral costs or bride prices, but again, I would advise you to do it as anonymously as possible, and as close to your departure date as possible. I have heard of a volunteer who spent his plane fare home on magnanimous gifts for everyone he knew. He is remembered as a fool in his sending agency and as a generous fool in the community he bestowed gifts to in Uganda.

TOO GOOD TO BE TRUE

There is also the very real problem of well-intentioned misinformation. In my experience here, local people just hate to be the bearer of bad news, and so go to considerable lengths to avoid communicating it. I hesitate to call it 'lying', as it isn't malicious, but for a researcher investigating impacts and perceptions, it can be very frustrating. Obviously, as I have spent longer here people have become more willing to tell things as they are. That is, in itself, an interesting phenomenon relating to perceptions, but be prepared to delve deep into stories that sound too good.

INHERITED REPUTATIONS

There is nothing much you can do about this, but as least you can be prepared for it. Wherever you are going will have had its own experience of *Muzungus* before you. You will be judged on their attitudes and behaviour, until you establish your own routine and personality in time. So, if you find that local people are suspicious of you, reluctant to talk to you, or just acting very off, it may not be all your own fault. Certainly, employ all your social skills of tact, respect, conversation and politeness (as you would anywhere), but if you are being persistently stonewalled, start enquiring about what other 'outsiders' have been there before. In my own case, I have been preceded by a variety of American volunteers, each leaving their own indelible mark on local peoples' perception of me, even before I arrived. It has taken a full year to correct some very grave misconceptions - hopefully you can achieve this more quickly.

'BEING WITH THE PEOPLE'

It is quite likely that you will be spending much time with the local people of the area where your study is based. No matter what support networks you establish for communication with home, these are the people with whom you will spend most of your working and leisure time. There is a phrase often used by volunteers and aid-workers in particular, of 'being with the people'. This implies that to live in the villages, eat and drink with local people and effectively shun association with other 'outsiders' in the area, is somehow 'better', 'more realistic' and certainly more politically correct than to be seen in town, drinking imported Heineken with your *Muzungu* friends. Obviously, there is a balance, and each person finds his/her own in time.

Other 'Outsiders'

Let me first deal with the 'outsider' community that you will decide to be part of, or not. As an independent researcher, you will have the advantage of not being associated with any particular group of 'outsiders' in the area, and you can effectively choose with whom to spend your time. Volunteers, aid-workers and other 'outsiders' are often submerged in the ex-pat culture that revolves around the small group of people with whom their predecessor lived. I have witnessed the extreme neo-colonialism of British ex-pat life in both Malaysia and Kampala and, to be honest, it came as a bigger shock to me than African cultures. Initially, I was quick to judge 'outsiders' on the 'altruism' of their occupation. Soon I discovered that NGOs with sterling reputations 'at home' often operate like extravagant private enterprises 'in the field'. Professional salaries with the big NGOs are ENORMOUS, tax-free, and are combined with the most amazing side-benefits. The ex-pat employees of the NGOs often live luxuriously in colossal houses, employing many local staff and buying exclusively from the 'Imports' shop in the city. I witnessed more racism among the ex-pats of the most laudable NGOs, than I ever did among the straightforward 'I'm-here-to-make-money' ex-pats. Also, strictly commercial enterprises often achieve as much in skills-training on a commercial basis, as a lengthy overseas aid project can hope to, on a charitable basis.

However, many high-salaried aid workers, business people and NGO workers were previously volunteers and remember well the difficulties that volunteers (student researchers) can face. This may make them more likely to give you some assistance. Try and draw on the knowledge of people who have lived in the area for some time, as they will have a wealth of experience that you may find useful. Even if you decide that you would never go near them in as million years at home, don't alienate yourself from them; chances are that you might need their established networks and contacts.

'The People'

And briefly, just a word on my first experience of living and working with people of a completely different culture. It sounds trite, and it certainly isn't an 'insight', but every day I am reminded of the fact that people are the same the world over. You will find people on your own wavelength, and if you can communicate well, good friendships will evolve. Also there are prats in every village, every town, every geography department in this world, so don't torture yourself with guilt for actually disliking some of the people you encounter in your fieldwork area. So, be prepared to have some of your pre-conceptions challenged - I certainly did.

COMMUNICATION

As well as locally-based contacts, you will want to have access to the 'outside world', both for general communication and also in cases of emergency.

Post

Generally, you are likely to be able to use a post office box at your nearest post office, where you can collect your mail. Either get your own (it shouldn't be too expensive), or, if you're not going to be in the area for a year, use somebody else's. Ask a local NGO office, mission, school or shop whether you can have mail sent to their box, and whether they will hold your mail.

Emergency Plans

On arriving at your fieldwork area, plan very soon how you would get out of there in a hurry. Sadly, it is a reality in East Africa and many other parts of the world, that civil disturbances are never very far from the surface, and you need to plan for the worst case scenario. For this reason, it is wise to be on friendly terms with people who have the means to travel - usually other 'outsiders'. Also, the information channels of NGOs in the area can get you information on the 'situation' that local people might not have access to. A combination of local information and 'outsider' information should enable you to make a decision about whether to remain or not. Sometimes one source is not reliable enough. The following account will give you some idea of what I mean.

Where I am located, in the very north-west of Uganda, my husband and I are the only two *Muzungus* in the county, so most of our information is local. We had heard rumours about the impending offensive by the Khartoum army on SPLA (Sudan People's Liberation Army) holdings in Southern Sudan, had seen some jets flying overhead, and were aware of some NRA (National Resistance Army) troop movement on the Ugandan side of the border, but our local friends weren't a bit bothered. We happened to be in Kampala when the offensive took place, and some

50,000 refugees were reported to be flooding across the border into Koboko, a town twenty miles north of our location in Maracha. There were tales of air strikes in our county, Sudanese manoeuvres into the West Nile and so on. We returned very quickly, despite the protests of *Muzungu* friends in Kampala. We found the mission to be as sleepy as ever and decided that the reports in Kampala had been exaggerated.

The next day, however, a Sudanese jet flew very low overhead and the first SPLA casualties were brought to the mission hospital. Suddenly, the mission and village were alive with tension and rumours - women were packing their few things to flee across the western border to Zaire, Sudanese Government 'spies' came and issued threats to the hospital, Red Cross tents were erected. Food aid started arriving and the dust on the road never had a chance to settle between the constant stream of UNHCR big-wigs whizzing past in their brand new Landcruisers. We listened to a variety of opinions from both local and expatriate friends, ranging from, 'If God wants us to die tomorrow, there's nothing we can do about it....' to, 'If I were you, I'd be gone already', and the inevitable 'Oh, this is NOTHING compared to what I went through in '79/'82/'87 etc.'. We decided to stay put, but made arrangements to borrow a vehicle if we had to leave quickly. We were able to base our decision on a variety of opinions; generally, local friends advised us to do nothing (but then they didn't understand that our parents would be climbing the walls, thinking we were in a war-zone), while Kampala friends advised us to get out of the West Nile for good. My point is, try to establish both networks of contacts and information, and make a contingency plan for leaving your area before you hope to.

Fast News

The other side of the coin is that you should establish contact channels so that people can get information to you in a hurry if need be. If you are in an urban area, you may have access to a telephone (or even fax!), and you should use the facilities of your academic contact, if possible. Leave a contact number with your department at home, and your nearest and dearest - for emergency use only. Of course, if you have an e-mail connection, this makes communications even easier. If, however, you are in the middle of nowhere, this may be out of the question. My nearest telephone is seven hours away, and I don't even have a vehicle to get there. Post takes two to three weeks (but is reliable), so I am okay for ordinary correspondence and planned phone calls. However, should somebody at home wish to contact me urgently, the procedure involves telephoning/faxing the 'Mother House' of a religious congregation in Kampala, who have members in the West Nile. The Mother House communicates by radio daily and, if the members in the West Nile tune in, the message can reach here within a day or two. If a local member of the congregation is passing through our mission here, I can receive the message in two-three days minimum. Even this isn't totally reliable. The fact that the congregation itself is primarily Italian means that the message is translated a few times and can evolve into a completely different one, or at best, a strange one. Recently, it took three days for news of the death of a volunteer colleague in Kenya to reach us here, and even then, we got the wrong name!

No matter how woeful the communication links seem at first, there is usually a means, perhaps unconventional, of receiving urgent news fairly quickly. Again, establish and use your *Muzungu* contacts to find out the best communication network, and then let a few people at home know how to use it. Religious congregations are usually very willing to help, and have considerable experience and advice to offer on the local area. Such congregations tend to have a long history in the area, staying there in times of trouble, when even the relief agencies have pulled out. I know several volunteers who have balked at the idea of approaching a community of fathers/brother/sisters, not coming from a religious background themselves, and who have been pleasantly surprised at the gentle welcome they received. Regardless of your background, it is another communications/support avenue which you might like to explore.

AND TO CONCLUDE...

Finally, a quick word about looking after yourself. Follow the advice given by your college health centre, and carry <u>Where There Is No Doctor</u>, as a first aid manual. DO bring clean syringes and needles. In your fieldwork area, be careful with the water particularly. No matter how much you want to 'be with the people' - I wouldn't advise that you drink the 'local brew' (be it cassava-, millet- or maize-based) until you've been in the area for a while. Ask around about who makes the 'cleanest' brew, and just take it easy until your stomach can cope.

Much of what I've said may apply only to Uganda or East Africa, but I would just like to stress again the importance of establishing contacts with other 'outsiders' in the area. Of course, try to learn the local language - at least the greetings and pleasantries, which seem to make up half of each conversation anyway. Don't push yourself too hard. Accept that a lifetime of western living HAS made you a bit of a softy, and don't go walking three miles to the local borehole on your first morning there. Accept help if it is offered; soon enough you will be able to repay kindnesses shown to you. Don't worry too much if you have a really rotten day, and feel like Spaceman Spiff on another planet - remember - you have days like that at home too.

Finally, if it all gets on top of you; the local elders have decided you're not to be trusted; your motorbike has packed up again; your research assistant has run off with your laptop computer and you've had the runs for a fortnight.......GO HOME! You're a student not a martyr, and you can always change the thesis title to suit your experience...can't you?

Good Luck!

Nuala Bryce Gormley

REFERENCES
Potter, Rob 1993 'Little England and little geography: reflections on Third World teaching and research', <u>Area</u> 25, 3, 291-294.

Sidaway, James 1992 'In other worlds: on the politics of research by 'First World' geographers in the 'Third World'', <u>Area</u> 24, 4, 403-410.

Werner, David <u>Where There is No Doctor</u> London: Macmillan. (copies available from Teaching Aids at Low Cost, Institute of Child Health, 30 Guildford Street, London, WC1N 1EH.)

PART II

PRACTICAL TIPS

Elsbeth Robson and **Katie Willis** with **Becky Elmhirst**

9.

LOOKING AFTER YOURSELF: HEALTH ISSUES

BEFORE YOU GO

1. The main piece of advice regarding health when carrying out fieldwork, is to go and see your doctor as soon as possible to explain your plans and ask about vaccinations and other requirements. This is vital, as you will probably need a course of inoculations over a period of weeks or months.

2. If you are taking any prescribed medication, take enough with you because replenishments may not be readily available. Just in case you need more and can answer any queries about the drugs you are carrying, make sure that you know the generic name of the drug, as trade names differ from country to country. Always carry the medicines in the container it was issued in. The Department of Health suggests that you also take a letter from your doctor or a copy of the prescription to avoid problems at customs if you are questioned about any pharmaceuticals you are carrying.

3. Have a check-up at the dentist and at the opticians (if appropriate) and act on their advice. If you wear glasses / contact lenses take a copy of your prescription with you and ensure you have a spare pair of glasses.

4. Make sure you know your blood group, just in case.

5. Buy, or assemble, a first aid kit and consider going on a first aid course, especially if you are going to be working in an isolated area. The St. John's Ambulance and the Red Cross run courses, and contacts for the local branch can be found in the phone book. Take advice from your doctor and, if possible, people who have worked in your fieldwork area, about what your first aid kit should include. You could also buy a dental first aid kit to deal with emergencies in the field. Interhealth provides a rapid mail order service for medical equipment and literature. (Addresses are in Chapter 13 *Useful References*). You may also want to read up on health issues before you leave - most travel guides include sections on health (see also the health section on the reading list at the end of this volume).

6. Take out health insurance. This is crucial, both to pay for any treatment that may be necessary and also for flying you home early if you become seriously ill or injured. Shop around for travel insurance and make sure that the policy you choose is appropriate for your needs and provides

sufficient cover. All providers of student insurance, travel agents and banks will be able to provide information about travel insurance (see further discussion in Chapter 10 *Safety and Insurance*).

7. Mosquitoes and malaria - if your doctor advises you to take malaria tablets, make sure that you start taking them before you leave and that you have sufficient tablets for your entire fieldwork visit and keep taking them for a month after your return. There are periodic changes in the recommended brands of malaria tablets, so get the latest medical advice. Remember to buy a mosquito net if appropriate (easily available in camping and outdoor shops) and treat it with repellent before you leave. Take advice as to the availability of insect repellent and the most effective formula. There may be a locally-available brand, which may be particularly effective. Mosquito repellent comes in various forms - there are creams and roll-ons to keep them away from you, stuff to treat your clothes with to make them repellent too, as well as spray, coils and tablets to burn to kill any mosquitoes in a closed room. You may need to tackle them on all fronts!

DURING FIELDWORK
1. As soon as you arrive, familiarise yourself with the local medical system. Where is the nearest doctor and pharmacy?

2. Food and Drink. Be careful! A change of diet can often lead to problems. Do not go around sampling everything in sight on your arrival, especially if local cuisine tends to be spicier then you are used to. A slow and steady transition period will reduce the likelihood of stomach upsets during the first few weeks.

'Bob quickly learnt to his cost that 'fresh' meant something entirely different'

Throughout your fieldwork take care with what you eat, but beware of becoming completely paranoid! Avoid unboiled water or ice, and also take precautions with unwashed vegetables, unpeeled fruit and reheated food. However, you should make sure that you maintain a balanced diet, so eradicating fruit and vegetables altogether on the grounds that they are 'dangerous' could lead to vitamin and mineral deficiency unless you take supplements in the form of vitamin pills. This should not be necessary, as with a bit of care, it is easy to eat all sorts of food, without any problems.

If you do not have access to safe water, you can sterilise water in a number of ways. Sterilising tablets are effective, cheap and easily available to take with you, but they tend to make the water taste horrible. Boiling and filtering water also makes it safer to drink. Sophisticated water filter gadgets are available from camping and outdoor equipment shops, but they have a limited capacity. If you are preparing vegetables at home, then they can be made safe by cleaning the dirt off them, peeling where possible and either cooking thoroughly, or sterilising. Fruit should be cleaned, then sterilised and peeled. Peeling an unwashed piece of fruit, apart from bananas, merely transfers the germs inwards. To sterilise fruit and vegetables use tincture of iodine or sterilising tablets at three times the dose normally used for water decontamination.

If you do get diarrhoea, keep drinking lots of liquids, rest and keep out of the sun. You might also want to take anti-diarrhoea tablets. Your doctor or pharmacist will be able to advise you on the best brands. If your condition does not improve after a few days, you may have dysentery and should see a doctor.

3. AIDS. There are very few parts of the world where AIDS cases have not been reported. You should, therefore, avoid putting yourself at risk of being infected with HIV. If you have to have an injection or stitches ensure that a clean needle is used. You can buy clean syringes and needles before you go - they are easily available in a sealed 'anti-AIDS' pack from a good chemist and should be labelled with your blood group and included in your first aid kit. It may be advisable to take a letter from your doctor explaining why you are carrying this medical equipment, translated into the local language if necessary, to avoid problems at customs. Locally-produced condoms may not meet the required standards to reduce the risk of HIV-transference, so you may want to take a supply of reliable ones with you.

4. Rabies. If you are going to an area where rabies is endemic, make sure that you have a course of rabies injections before you go. These will not make you immune to rabies, but will give you more time in which to seek

medical attention if you are bitten, scratched or licked by a rabid animal. A big stick or a few rocks are always useful, if you are walking around areas where animals are likely to be infected. If you are bitten, wash the wound and seek medical help immediately.

5. Sun. If you are travelling in bright sunshine, cover your head, use sun-screen and drink lots of liquids to avoid dehydration. Sun-screen can be expensive or unobtainable in some places, so ensure that you have a supply with you before you leave.

6. Swimming. Always take local advice about safe places to swim. In some countries, especially in Sub-Saharan Africa, water-borne diseases, such as bilharzia, are common. So the only safe places to swim are the sea, as long as you are aware of potentially dangerous tides and currents, and properly maintained swimming pools.

ON YOUR RETURN

If you have been ill during your fieldwork, make sure that you have a thorough check-up when you get back. You should also be aware, that certain conditions can reappear or flair up, long after your return and may not be immediately recognisable, so always keep your doctor informed of your travels. Don't forget to keep on taking the malaria tablets for the recommended period after fieldwork.

10.

TAKING CARE AND JUST IN CASE: SAFETY AND INSURANCE[1]

Matters of safety and insurance when undertaking fieldwork are of concern both to physical and human geographers, but perhaps in different ways. Obviously what is 'safe', or 'unsafe', varies from place to place and from person to person; so this section is not intended to be unduly alarming, but it is hoped that a few common sense points of advice may be helpful. Please keep in mind that while most postgraduates may have one or two bad experiences, few get into really serious trouble. Geographers may find themselves working in dangerous, or potentially dangerous, environments; while cliffs and crevasses can present risks to fieldworkers, so can civil disorder and political crisis.

It should be remembered that in the field your safety is your own responsibility and it is your prime responsibility. No rock sample, interview, or photograph, is worth risking life and limb for. Think carefully before doing anything foolhardy. Is it safe to go out at night? Should you work alone, or with others? Most postgraduates inevitably work alone which can increase risks. Think and ask 'is it safe?' before you go ahead. If in doubt don't! It is important to keep a sensible perspective - your supervisor and family are probably on the other side of the world, so it's up to you. But keep a responsible person locally informed of your plans and whereabouts so that if you 'disappear' they can be alerted to your absence. Obviously before you go, you need to get the right sort of training for the kind of environment you will work in e.g. mountaineering skills if you're heading for the Himalayas, desert survival skills for the Sahara; get street wise if it's the neighbourhoods of Calcutta; learn to scuba dive if you're collecting corals off the Great Barrier Reef.

INSURANCE
Taking out adequate insurance in advance of your fieldwork is too important to ignore. The cost of insurance should be included in any research budget submitted in application for funds. ISIS is a well known provider of student insurance services which can be obtained from

---

[1] This section has been expanded since the first edition, largely due to the inclusion of Becky Elmhirst's discussion of road safety.

Endsleigh Insurance Services[2], or STA Travel who have offices on most campuses in the U.K. Endsleigh provide specific packages designed for students travelling and studying abroad and is available for anyone up to age 65. But check that the policy covers any expensive equipment you may need to take with you. Another possibility is to take out insurance from your travel agent in conjunction with an air ticket. Check that cover is adequate and it is reasonably priced because it may be designed for short tourist trips rather than a longer stay. If you are planning to drive while doing fieldwork you need to check out and make sure you have adequate insurance - for the car and you in case of an accident.

If you need to make an insurance claim of any kind you will almost certainly need a police report of theft, or loss, and evidence of hospital, or medical, bills. Let the insurers know what has happened as soon as possible - write to them from the field and keep photocopies of all the documentation and correspondence. When dealing with police and other officials be courteous - it often helps to smile and use formal forms of address like 'Sir' or 'Officer'. It might be a good idea to take a 'local' with you and stress that you only want to report a theft, or loss - not that you need them to do anything except acknowledge your report in writing. Avoid losing your temper except when really necessary.

LOCAL ADVICE

It is always a good idea to take advice from people on the ground who know the situation better than you do, but do not be too hesitant about exploring and evaluating local opinion. Sally Lloyd Evans' research into the informal sector in Trinidad necessitated working in low-income communities of Port of Spain. At the nearby university she was given repeated advice about the dangers of working with poor workers in the informal sector. In particular, strict warnings were given not to go into an informal market known as 'the People's Mall', or the 'Drag Mall', which was run by a group of Rastafarian traders. Initially, she heeded advice given by university colleagues until a local social worker suggested that fear of the Mall was based more on differences in class and ethnicity, than on any real danger. In Sally's subsequent experience the Mall turned out to be a much safer environment than the image of the place held by university colleagues whose socialisation prevented them from being familiar with those communities. In this kind of way, as outsiders, visiting postgraduates are often able to work around social boundaries and local prejudices.

---

[2] The address is given in Chapter 13.

TAKING CARE OF VALUABLES

In many societies where deprivation and crime are commonplace, outsiders (especially those perceived as 'rich') may be a vulnerable target. An obvious safety tip to deter all kinds of theft and muggings is to avoid taking any unnecessary valuables with you on fieldwork. If you flaunt obvious wealth where there is poverty, someone may understandably want to relieve you of your possessions. Easy preventative measures are confidence and knowing the area, as well as hiding money and valuable articles.

'Bob couldn't help showing off his expensive new toys'

It should go without saying that passport, tickets, travellers cheques, credit cards, money etc. should be kept safe. Make sure you have their details in several places. Leave numbers of travellers cheques and credit cards at home before departure, as well as photocopies of your passport and ticket. When travelling keep them on your person in a money belt, waist bag, or neck purse. Do not sort out their contents in public - retreat to the nearest toilet if necessary. Don't leave valuables in hotel or guest house rooms even if you are sure you have the only key. It may be better to leave them with the management - but use your judgement. If you are carrying money and documents with you it makes sense to spread them about your person - don't forget secure places like tucked inside a shoe or bra.

Think about your valuables. For instance do you really need to wear that gold-plated family heirloom watch? Why not get a cheap watch? Then it will not be a major disaster if it gets stolen, or you give it away as a gift, or even as a bribe. Expensive jewellery is also usually unnecessary and can be at risk of theft. But don't necessarily go without any jewellery. Wearing jewellery can make you feel good in yourself. In many cultures jewellery is an important part of local dress and can help you to 'fit in'. You may be able to buy cheap local jewellery which is not out of place. Expensive looking jewellery may place you in a certain class - so wearing it, or not wearing it, can make a significant difference to how people perceive and relate to you. If you want to ingratiate yourself to the élite social classes it doesn't have to be real gold - flashy costume jewellery can do just as well, but be warned that in hot and sweaty environments gold plate can quickly wear off! In many places the appropriate dress and accessories can make you feel more comfortable and prevent unnecessary harassment, or unwanted attention.

Context is all important to the matter of dress and safety. For example, Elsbeth Robson reports that when she was in Nigeria she was in the situation where it was highly appropriate to wear lots of gold jewellery when invited to weddings and other social events of the educated urban élite. Yet she did not feel that she could assure the safety of such belongings in the place where she was living and also could not afford such expensive items. Consequently, she constantly felt underdressed although she adopted local dress to the extent that it was within her means. Yet at the same time when conducting research in the village expensive jewellery would have been totally inappropriate because of the rural setting.

TAKING CARE OF YOURSELF - PERSONAL SECURITY
To avoid trouble with authorities when working overseas make sure you have all the necessary research permissions. It is also often a good idea to make sure you carry identification with you all the time - photocopy the relevant pages of your passport, or carry a student card, or a letter from your university/affiliated institution in the host country explaining who you are and what you are doing. These concerns of personal safety to 'keep out of trouble' also extend to considerations of potential political instability. It

is sensible to be aware that in some parts of the world sensitive political situations can turn into a state of emergency overnight. Follow the news on the BBC World Service and in local media so you are aware of any serious situations. Register with your embassy, or consulate, even if you are not interested in cocktail parties and expatriate social life. It may be useful to register with them while you are resident in the country so that in the event of an emergency, or disaster, they may be in a position to offer assistance.[3]

If difficult political situations do arise research plans may need to be adapted. For example, two months before Sally Lloyd Evans was due to embark on field research in Trinidad there was an attempted coup in the country leading to a six month state of emergency. Acting on instructions from the Foreign and Commonwealth Office[4], the fieldtrip was postponed for six months and the research agenda altered. After much personal insistence permission was given to travel to Trinidad in January 1991. Situations like this rarely happen, but in the unlikely event that they do it is important to be adaptable. Be assured that most problems usually work out eventually.

In matters of personal security, it is perhaps sensible to be cautious. Issues of personal safety apply to all researchers - men as well as women. In general it is important to be aware of social conventions of dress and behaviour in the country you visit. For example, in some places women wearing trousers or 'immodest' clothing may be assumed to be prostitutes. Women moving about or travelling alone may also be vulnerable and it may not be considered socially acceptable for women to go alone to places like bars, or liquor stores. Also be careful when making new contacts. You should also consider how your research topic may be interpreted. For example, Gill Green *at al.* (1993) highlight how sex research can be thought to be 'provocative' "and may be used as an excuse for sexual harassment" (p.627).[5] Use your better judgement and err on the side of caution to avoid situations where you may feel unsafe. Don't get into situations alone with a stranger if you feel uncomfortable.

There is no basis for any ideas that women occupy a disadvantaged position for carrying out fieldwork because they are more at risk. In some communities where there is a collective sense of 'sisterhood', such as the Caribbean, there is often an immediate collaborative system open to women on the basis of their gender. Even in so-called *macho* societies where women are generally regarded as occupying a subservient role, female researchers can take advantage of the traditional roles of women.

---

[3] This is also discussed by Nuala Bryce Gormley in her chapter.
[4] The address of the Foreign and Commonwealth Office is given in Chapter 13.
[5] Although their discussion is based on research in the UK, similar issues need to be considered when working in 'developing areas'.

For example, women researchers often find themselves disregarded as important, or a potential threat, by local communities, especially by their men and local authorities like police. A woman researcher may well be freer to wander around without raising any suspicion over her presence as an outsider. Male outsiders, however, might provoke questions about what they are doing and who they work for. However, while women may find it easier to interact informally with local communities they may also find it difficult to be taken seriously by male officials, or academics. With determination and effort this problem can be overcome.

To avoid theft or personal attack in big cities moving about clearly without jewellery, watch, or camera you will feel less threatened. Learn to move defensively - avoid eye contact, be aware of what's going on around, keep your hands in your pockets, or on your bag, know where you're going and keep moving purposively. You may be happier not to travel, or move about, alone, but conversely a gaggle of outsiders may attract unsought attention. When you first arrive in a place be cautious and alert until you get the feel of the environment. When travelling it helps sometimes to establish rapport with fellow passengers who are likely to be just as concerned as you about their comfort and the safety of themselves and their belongings. Try exchanging greetings, passing the time of day, sharing sweets or cigarettes. But exercise caution in accepting refreshments - travellers have been drugged and their possessions stolen after drinking laced orange juice.

If, in the hopefully highly unlikely event, you are harassed, or assaulted, your first priority is to seek a safe environment and someone you trust. A friend, a colleague, or an organisation may be able to offer you the help and guidance you need to deal with things like contacting the police, seeking medical treatment (including counselling), pursuing legal action, informing your supervisor and family, deciding whether and how to pursue the field work.

TOWARDS A ROAD SAFETY CODE[6]

For most people, weighing up the dangers of fieldwork in a developing country usually involves some examination of the possibility of illness, the risk of a natural disaster, the likelihood of social unrest and thinking through the steps needed to ensure personal safety when working alone in the field. One danger that is rarely mentioned, and that should be considered wherever you are undertaking fieldwork, is that of road traffic accidents. Perhaps because there is no vaccination against road accidents, and maybe because road travel is pretty well unavoidable in field research

---

[6] This section was written by Becky Elmhirst.

(unless you opt for solely archival, or computer-based research), the possibility that one might die or be seriously injured in a road accident is just never written into the fieldwork planning equation. Yet statistics, and my own personal experience, suggest to me that this is a foolish course to take as road travel in developing countries involves very real dangers which you should be aware of.[7]

A recent World Health Organisation report claims that in 1990 road traffic accidents ranked ninth (equal with tuberculosis) in the international tables of causes of death and disability (WHO, 1996). The situation is particularly serious in developing countries where fatalities per 10,000 vehicles per year are as many as 180 (Ethiopia) compared to less than five (UK). Furthermore, it is in those developing countries that under-resourced emergency services and hospital care are least likely to be able to deal with the aftermath of a major traffic smash. Until recently, I had been just as casual about road accidents as most other researchers. My pre-fieldwork worries (apart from data anxiety) concerned malaria, snake bites and hassles the female researcher might expect when working alone. I had been around enough to know that bus journeys were usually marked by a few hair-raising incidents, the stuff of travellers' tales, in fact. It was in this spirit that road accidents were discussed at language school prior to fieldwork. My fellow students and I had joked nervously about some gruesome statistic that at least two of us would be heading home earlier than intended, the latest victims of Indonesia's terrifying roads. Looking back, that conversation has an ominous ring to it, as twelve months later, I found myself to be one of the two (the other, an Australian volunteer, was not so lucky - he lost his life in a motorcycle accident on Sulawesi). What happened to me led to my re-evaluating how to conduct fieldwork, and to devising my own fieldwork safety code for damage limitation, which has subsequently guided my fieldwork decision-making.

I was travelling back to my Sumatran research site after a short break in the city, when the public bus on which I was travelling, went out of control and off the road, rolling over and over into a ditch. My recollection of what happened is only vague, but suffice it to say I was lucky enough to come out with a few broken bones and minor cuts, while many others were killed. At the time, the first thing I did was to break open my first aid kit and share out sterile swabs and packets of sterile water to mop up cuts. I was later told that this had saved me from suffering severe serious complications (including gangrene) associated with

---

[7] Readers may also be aware that Kevin Phillips-Howard from Department of Geography, University of Transkei, Umtata, South Africa was killed in a car crash in October 1995. He had long-standing links with the Department of Geography, University of Durham.

puncture wounds. Item 1 in my code, therefore, has been always to carry a medical kit even for the shortest journeys, and even where airline baggage allowances suggest leaving such items at home.

The next problem was getting from the scene of the accident (miles from anywhere) back to the city. I was lucky enough to have my faculties intact, and my functional fluency in Bahasa Indonesia and a wodge of cash persuaded a passing truck driver to get to hospital. Item 2 in the code: always carry enough cash to get out of a scrape, and learn the language. I spent a night in hospital (hooked up to a drip, courtesy of the sterile medical kit I had brought and never thought I would use), and it was decided that I should go back to the UK for the necessary operations. Although I had full medical insurance, I ended up relying on friends I had got to know in the city, who provided me with a place to stay, helped me arrange flights and exit visas and packed my bags for me (I didn't have the use of my arms). Item 3 in my code and probably the most important, is make sure you have a good support network close to your fieldsite, so you can get out of difficulties. Friends can take on what even the best medical insurance does not cover, including actually telephoning the emergency number (which I had not even thought of given my confusion).

It took me several months (and several operations) before I recovered from my injuries. In the months that followed the accident, I learned much about road accidents overseas as I shared my experiences with others who had done fieldwork, and I began to discover just how common they are. For example, one of my colleagues in Indonesia was thrown from the back of a lorry which crashed on the way from his fieldsite in the Sudan. An anthropologist I met at a conference had been on a bus that went over a cliff (miraculously no one was hurt), and a friend broke both arms and legs in a motorcycle accident in the Philippines. According to Nancy Howell (1990), one in four field researchers are involved in some sort of road accident. When we spoke to her to check this figure for an article that appeared in *New Scientist* (Elmhirst, 1996; Seymore, 1996), she told us that she had been prompted to research and write her book after the death of her own son while doing his doctoral fieldwork.

What has struck me about all the stories I have heard is that they all involve field researchers on limited budgets who have necessarily chosen the cheapest form of travel: usually buses (in which over-tired drivers attempting to meet unrealistic journey times make mistakes), or motorcycles (which leave the rider vulnerable to the vagaries of the road). Few of the horror stories I have heard involved World Bank officials in air-conditioned Land Cruisers. Suffice it to say that there is a political economy to road traffic accidents and one which fieldwork budgeting does well to take into account. The fourth item in my damage limitation code is, therefore, to cost out the true costs of fieldwork travel, and take into account the higher risk associated with motorcycles and public buses, compared to the hire of a jeep.

Clearly, a fieldwork road safety code is hardly enough to prevent the accident ever happening. However, unless you are prepared to give up the idea of fieldwork altogether, there is little alternative but to take steps to avoid situations being more serious than they need be. My belief is that these should form part and parcel of fieldwork logistics wherever in the world you plan to work.

CONCLUSIONS

The aim of this section was not to scare you off fieldwork, but rather to highlight some of the issues that you should be aware of, and to provide suggested strategies for dealing with potential problems. For most people, fieldwork is one of the best times of their lives, and will sufficient preparation it probably will be for you too!

REFERENCES

Elmhirst, Becky 1996 'The newest demon' New Scientist 151, 14 September, 36.

Green, Gill, Rosaline S. Barbour, Marina Barnard & Jenny Kitzinger (1993) 'Who wears the trousers?: Sexual harassment in research settings', Women's Studies International Forum 16,6, 627-637.

Howell, Nancy 1990 Surviving Fieldwork Washington DC: American Anthropological Association.

Seymore, Jane 1996 'Trafficking in death' New Scientist 151, 2047, 14 September, 34-37.

WHO 1996 Investing in Health Research and Development Washington DC: World Health Organisation.

11.

FROM MONEY TO MOSQUITO NETS: IDEAS FOR PACKING YOUR RUCKSACK

The main piece of advice about what to take with you for an extended fieldwork trip is 'keep it simple'. Decide what bag/suitcase/rucksack you are going to use - if everything does not fit into it, then you will have to leave things behind. Do not be tempted to get a bigger bag, unless you are having to contemplate discarding things that are vital for your research. Have a packing trial run about a week before you leave - otherwise the night before could be spent having last-minute rationalisation dilemmas. Remember that exceeding airline baggage allowances, if your luggage is too heavy or consists of too many items, can be very expensive.

Everybody will have different needs to meet their requirements, so a definitive guide to what to take and what not to take is impossible. However, we feel that there are a number of issues that should be considered regarding equipment, regardless of specific personal requirements.

BAGGAGE

Baggage should be strong, sturdy, preferably lockable regardless of where you are going and what you are doing. Just in case it should go astray luggage should always be labelled with home and destination addresses. When choosing what type of luggage to take, make sure you consider how you are going to be travelling and how far you will have to carry it!

Keeping your baggage to a minimum is a good idea as travelling is a big enough headache, without having to deal with large numbers of bags. However, if you do find that you have excess baggage, you will have to choose how to transport it. This is usually the case on the way back from fieldwork, when you have amassed large amounts of data, books and samples. If everything in your luggage is immediately necessary, then you will have to cough up the money for excess baggage, but if you feel that there are things that you could do without for a few weeks or even months, for example, books and clothes, then you should consider sending them by freight or as cargo which is cheaper. Some airlines have reasonable rates for unaccompanied baggage or cargo.

If at all possible, copy your data, for example coding sheets, interview tapes or information on computer discs, and send them by post, so that even if all your luggage is lost, you will have something to work with on your return.

CLOTHES

When deciding what clothes to take, you need to take into consideration factors including climate, the type of work that you will be doing, local dress codes, space in your luggage and the availability of suitable clothing in the field. You should also be aware that many funding bodies will pay for items of specialised clothing needed for fieldwork. This may range from waterproofs for work in tropical or monsoon climates, to a suit if you have to carry out formal interviews with politicians etc. In most fieldwork situations, being at the height of fashion is not important, so it is a good idea to concentrate on cheap, easily washable clothes. Perhaps even clothes you would be happy to give away as gifts and will not be too distressed about if they fade in the sun, become permanently stained by mud in the rainy season or tear from being washed by hand.

'Going to the tropics Bob only thought to pack his holiday clothes'

TOILETRIES

If you cannot contemplate surviving without a certain brand of face cream, shampoo etc., then make sure that you stock up before you go, in case it is unobtainable in the field. Other items that will probably be difficult to obtain, or will be very expensive include, contact lens solution, tampons and sun cream. Try and find out what is available before you go.

COMPUTERS

As the use of computers has become increasingly widespread for data manipulation and graphics, as well as for basic word processing, the question of access to computers in the field has become more relevant. If you are used to using a computer on a regular basis, being deprived of one during your fieldwork could prove to be decidedly inconvenient. Even if you do not use a computer regularly, you may feel that being able to enter data directly into a computer while in the field could be a great advantage, saving both time and energy on your return.

If you decide that a computer is necessary, your next step is to investigate the availability of computing facilities. If you are going to be attached to a university or research institute in the field, then you may be able to use computers there. However, be warned that computer resources are often limited and there are the added problems of compatibility of both hard and software, accessibility and problems with the power supply.

You may decide that you need to take a computer with you. Some departments have portable computers to loan out to researchers, but in most cases you will have to buy one yourself and unfortunately few grant-giving bodies will support computer purchases. Although portable computers can run on batteries, remember that their life span is a matter of three to five hours, so you will have to recharge them or run your computer from the mains. It is vital, therefore, to ensure that the local electricity supply is compatible with your machine. You might need a particular adapter or transformer and may need to protect your equipment from power cuts and fluctuations with a stabiliser. Using an adapter you can run a computer from a car lighter socket or with a bit of ingenuity, you might be able to run your computer directly off a car battery. Adapters cost about £100 and can be purchased from most computer suppliers. Solar panels for computer battery recharge are also available - check the ads in computer magazines.

As well as your computer, you should also take a supply of floppy discs, spare cartridges and maybe even sheet feed paper if you are taking a printer, because these items may be very expensive or unobtainable in the field. As always, remember to back up your discs before you go and at regular intervals during your stay.

CAMERAS

Most students take cameras with them when they embark on fieldwork. Before you go, you should decide what you want to take pictures for, as this will influence the type of camera and film that you take. If you just want to take snapshots of places and people you visit, then an inexpensive camera will suffice. However, if photographs are going to play an important role in your research, then something more sophisticated might be necessary. If you want to make slides from your pictures, you will have to buy slide film and always make sure that you buy film of the correct exposure for your needs. Similar preparations need to be made if you are taking a video camera.

Some departments provide film and developing services for researchers. Find out if this applies to your department. When applying for funds, remember to include photographic costs in your budget outline. Think about arrangements for developing your films. Will it be a long time before they can be developed, if you are in a remote area perhaps. Films kept in a fridge or cool conditions are less likely to deteriorate over time. What are the pros and cons of developing the films while in the field compared with bringing or sending them back? These may involve considerations of cost, convenience and picture quality. For example, developing pictures in the fieldwork location means it is easier to give photographs as presents, but the quality of developing may be poorer.

When crossing international boundaries, it is a good idea to avoid having a film loaded in your camera as customs officials may want to look inside. Most airport x-ray machines now claim to be safe for films, but do not assume this to be the case if there is no sign. You could end up losing all your photographic masterpieces.

TAPE RECORDERS

You may want a tape recorder in order to tape interviews. If so, you should consider if this is appropriate and possible.[1] If the answer to these questions is 'yes', then you will have to decide what type of tape recorder to take with you. Depending on the work you are doing, you may want to take a small hand-held machine, or alternatively, a larger device with a microphone attached. Always make sure that you take sufficient tapes and batteries and that if you intend to run the tape recorder from the mains, that the electricity supply is compatible and you have the right kind of plug or adapter.

---

[1] Sarah Howard discusses tape recording in her chapter.

Even if your work does not involve interviews, you may want to take a tape recorder to provide music for those long nights when you're writing up your fieldnotes (see below).

CALCULATOR
If appropriate, consider taking a solar-powered calculator as it saves on batteries. If it is a cheap model, it can make a good present when leaving.

PHYSICAL GEOGRAPHY EQUIPMENT
Take advice as to what you should take and avoid carrying bulky pieces of equipment if at all necessary. Make sure that everything is packed securely, but that boxes can be opened easily, if customs officials want to examine the contents. You may need customs clearance for some equipment or samples, so make enquiries. Take into account the time it may take for equipment and/or samples to be transported to and from the field area - customs clearance can be a very lengthy procedure.[2]

PRESENTS
Depending on the type of research you are doing, you may want to take presents for key informants. Small, light articles are ideal and could include postcards, pens or other 'souvenirs'. Another aspect of reciprocity is being willing to share information about your family and friends and life 'at home'. Photographs are very useful when describing people and places, so you might want to put a few well-chosen pictures in your luggage.

KEEPING SANE
Although you will be working for much of your time in the field, you will have some time off and you should give some thought to things you need to take for your leisure time - you might want some 'luxuries' for your periods of relaxation. As far as equipment goes, the main things to consider here are kettles and music! If you cannot live without a hot drink at regular intervals, and you are going to have access to an electricity supply, consider taking a travel kettle or element to heat water. If you do not have cooking facilities, a kettle can also boil eggs and even cook rice or noodles.

Given that you may be spending a great deal of time on your own, a short-wave radio can be a great way of keeping in touch with both local and international news and whiling away the hours. A personal stereo can prevent severe boredom setting in on long journeys, but you should take

---

[2] For more information see the chapter by Georgina Endfield and Peter O'Connor.

care, as their use is not always socially appropriate. Buying and listening to local music cassettes is also a great way to explore local culture.

INSURANCE & MONEY

Remember to take out insurance that covers all your electrical items as well as your possessions in general. Some policies exclude expensive items, such as computers. If you do not have a credit card, you might want to consider getting one, just in case of emergencies. If you run out of money you can obtain cash advances on your credit card, although this will not be possible in all countries, so make specific enquiries about your destination. Other ways of obtaining money while in the field are discussed in Chapter 12 *Life in the Field.*

12.

KEEPING SANE: LIFE IN THE FIELD

One of the main motivations for producing this monograph, was to give prospective fieldworkers some advice which is not covered in the usual textbooks or supervisors' comments. This is especially true when it comes to questions regarding everyday life in the field. You will, hopefully, spend much of your time working, but you should also give some thought to what are you going to do in your spare time and how are you going to keep in touch with family, friends and the rest of the world in general.

ON ARRIVAL
When you arrive at your fieldwork destination, there is the understandable urge to dive in and to get on with all the interviews and research that you had planned with your supervisor. However, it is very important to take your time for a number of reasons. Firstly, your body needs time to get used to a new climate, food and time zone, as well as all the excitement of arriving in a new location.

Secondly, there is the need to get settled, find somewhere to live, find out where to buy food, locate a telephone/bank/post office etc. and meet up with any contacts you have. This all relies on getting to know the local area. Setting off with a local map (if there is any such map available) and wandering around is an ideal way to do this. You may also want to sit in a village/town square to get a feel for the place, but be aware of the way in which this could be interpreted and be sensitive and prepared for questions from local residents.

Finally, your research project, so lovingly crafted 'at home' will need to be reconsidered in the field. If you are intending to carry out a questionnaire survey or sampling, you will have to select study districts. The best way to do this is to walk around the area to find out what is suitable and also to talk to researchers at local universities etc. This will also be useful for talking over your fieldwork plans with people who know the area. However much you prepare before leaving, there are many things to do in the field when you arrive before it is possible to begin the actual data gathering.

It is, therefore, a good idea to set aside time at the beginning of your stay for 'settling in'. Avoid the urge to embark on 'formal' fieldwork straight away. You may save yourself time and effort in the long run, if you take stock of the situation at the start.

CULTURE SHOCK[1]

However much you have read about a place, however many TV programmes/films you have watched and however many people you have talked to, you are bound to feel 'culture shock' at some point during your fieldwork. Everybody will experience this in different ways as it is 'a vague individualistic phenomenon', but common signs include restlessness and depression, sporadic obsessions with things 'from home', especially food, and feelings of frustration, isolation and confusion at living in a different culture.

Oberg (1954) described four stages of culture shock and although such a clear progression through this cycle is not everyone's experience, it is a useful way of classifying the gamut of emotions through which the fieldworker moves. The 'Honeymoon Stage' is one of excitement at arrival at your destination with all the new ways of doing things waiting to be discovered. This is replaced by the 'Hostile Stage' where you begin to feel frustration and irritation with every aspect of daily routine. The 'Initial Recovery Stage' is characterised by humour and sarcasm, often incorporating feelings of superiority. Finally, you arrive at 'Adjustment' the stage in which you have accepted the 'new' culture and have adapted to changes. As Woodlief observes, in reality the chronological ordering of these emotions does not exist. Instead you can swing from one to the other in one day. However, what we would like to stress is that such feelings are not uncommon. Many fieldwork accounts give the impression that the researcher was able to slip effortlessly between 'home' and 'field', but this is rarely, if ever the case. Do not feel guilty if you long for your weekly dose of soap operas, get frustrated because you cannot get hold of the football results, or feel irritation at the amount of time you have to spend queuing up in banks. Your normal routine has been changed and you will take time to adjust.

MONEY

Banking systems vary throughout the world, but it is very unlikely that you will want to take and keep all your money with you in cash. You are, therefore, likely to have to use a bank at some point during your fieldwork. A common solution is to take a small amount of money in cash, preferably in small denomination notes and coins, and the rest in travellers' cheques. Before you go, take advice as to what sort of travellers' cheques are most

---

[1] This section draws greatly on Mari Woodlief (1990).

likely to be accepted. American Express and Visa cheques tend to be most widely welcomed, but the dollars or sterling question depends on your destination. For example, in Latin America sterling travellers' cheques are often regarded with great suspicion as the US dollar is the usual currency of international exchange in the region.

There is also the question of how to get money sent to you, especially if you are due to receive a grant instalment during your absence. Organising a third party mandate before you leave will enable somebody else to authorise the transfer of money from your account. As most funding agencies will only pay grants into your personal bank account, this is vital if you want to gain access to your money while you are away, as trying to deal with your local branch from thousands of miles away is virtually impossible.

Getting hold of the money in the field provides further problems. The ideal would probably be to open a bank account so money could be transferred, but many countries have restrictions regarding short-stay foreigners holding reserves in domestic banks, so this is often not possible and transfers can take a long time to materialise. There are, therefore, a number of possibilities including having money wired to a local bank, Western Union money transfers and American Express Moneygrams. All these will have local variations which should be checked before departure.

In emergencies, embassies are, in most cases, very unwilling to bail out their nationals. If you need money, therefore, you may have to arrange for money to be wired to you, or you may be able to use a credit card to obtain a cash advance, but in many remoter parts of the world credit cards are unheard of. It may be possible to write a sterling cheque from your home bank account for someone (possibly an ex-pat) who has a UK bank account and is willing to give you local currency in exchange.

SOCIAL LIFE

Living in a 'foreign' country for a prolonged period of time, is a wonderful opportunity and one which should be used to the full. Rather than spending all your time working, socialising and travelling is not only beneficial for your well-being, but can also help to contextualise your research.

Throughout the fieldwork period, you are likely to be invited to different kinds of social events, by a range of people. It is obviously advisable to be aware of the expectations involved and how you will be judged in terms of the company you keep, but this does not mean that a hermit-like existence is the solution. Sensitivity is one thing, over-cautious behaviour is another, although the line between the two is often blurred and can only be distinguished after experience in a particular environment. Take advice, and if you feel uncomfortable, do not accept. But to turn down an invitation to a family event like a wedding or a social gathering such as a village festival could be churlish and interpreted negatively - so think carefully.

Despite the amount of literature on the 'fieldwork experience' very little is written about pursuing romantic or intimate relationships 'in the field'.[2] 'Going out' with somebody from the local area will obviously affect your perceptions and relation to the local community, but it will also influence other people's behaviour towards you. On the one hand, you may be welcomed into different social spheres of because of your partner and you may also become the butt of friendly jokes about 'going native' etc. However, reactions may also be negative and could be related to perceptions regarding your greater wealth and opportunities. You may be regarded as having used your 'unfair advantage' to get a local boyfriend/girlfriend, or your partner may be ostracised because going out with you means crossing race/class/culture/religious boundaries and is interpreted as an indication that your local counterparts 'are not good enough'. Female researchers going out with local men are often characterised as being fools who have been taken in by their superficial charm; or the local community may be pleased and flattered that the woman outsider is coupled with one of their sons. Of course, any romantic relationship forged while 'in the field' faces an uncertain future in view of its long term possibilities but there are probably people who met their life partners in such conditions and many more who parted amicably when the time came and some who were broken hearted...

Many of these issues are similar for both heterosexual and homosexual relationships, however, in the case of gay relationships, local attitudes towards homosexuality may complicate matters further. Explicit opposition to your lifestyle may occur and you may find yourself unable to carry out research in a particular area. Whatever your sexual orientation, having an intimate personal relationship during fieldwork may affect the way people respond to your research questions. We are not saying that you should remain single throughout the fieldwork period or that each potential partner should be carefully analysed to ascertain their potential effect on your fieldwork (!), but you should be aware of the problems that may arise in certain contexts. Nonetheless it is our experience and belief that intense cross-cultural friendships can be very enriching for both parties.

Vegetarianism as a dietary preference is unknown in many parts of the 'Third World', although the enforced absence of meat in the diet due to economic reasons prevails widely. It is here that questions of the context

---

[2] Exceptions to this trend are Peter Wade (1993) and the volume edited by Don Kulick and Margaret Willson (1995).

of ethics, discussed by Clare Madge in her chapter, are specifically relevant. To some, choosing to eschew a meat-based diet is a luxury and one which can be interpreted both as 'western lunacy' or rudeness when a vegetarian is faced with a plate of meat in a 'Third World' setting. Because meat is regarded in many cultures as a luxury, to be offered it as a visitor is flattering, and as such a refusal to eat could be construed as a slight or snub. It is advisable, therefore, to consider how strong you hold your vegetarian beliefs and whether other issues become more important in particular settings. If you really cannot entertain the prospect of eating something, try and explain why rather than refusing it out of hand, or you could always plead illness.

HOMESICKNESS

In recent years, the construction of 'home' or notions of 'here' and 'there' have been increasingly addressed.[3] One of the themes of such work is that 'home' is only really identified and recognised once you are away from it. In the context of fieldwork, you will invariably miss family and friends, but 'home' may also be constructed in terms of research support and academic backup, as well as the whole context of landscape, food, politics, music, sport etc. This imagined home can feed homesickness but you will survive.

It is important to keep in contact with family, friends and supervisors in order to avoid the isolated feeling which may otherwise result. Before you leave for fieldwork, try and make everyone you know promise to write at least one letter during your long stay, as letters can provide a wonderful tonic during those lonely days in the field. If you do not have an address, then letters can be sent to the *post restante* in a town, or, if you are an American Express card holder and there is an office in your fieldwork area, letters can be sent there. Local NGOs may also be willing to hold your mail. (Other suggestions for receiving mail are given in Nuala Bryce Gormley's contribution).

You may also want friends and/or family to come and visit you in the field. This has numerous benefits for all concerned. Firstly, your isolation and homesickness can be alleviated by the arrival of visitors from 'home' (although their departure may leave you with a feeling of emptiness, or perhaps relief). Secondly, it enables your visitors to find out what you are actually doing by seeing the environment where you work, rather than relying on your descriptions and photographs. This can be especially important on your return 'home', when you will invariably feel 'homesick' for the field. Finally, having visitors helps put you in a context for local

---

[3] Such work includes Doreen Massey (1992), Biddy Martin and Chandra Talpade Mohanty (1986), George Robertson *et al.* (1994).

residents. Rather than being a 'foreign' individual, you become someone with a family and friends. (Elsbeth Robson discusses these issues in more detail in Chapter 4).

As well as keeping in contact with family and friends, you may also want to keep abreast of news from 'home'. Locally-produced newspapers may provide information about major world events, but for the more detailed news, you will have to look elsewhere. The BBC Radio World Service provides good coverage of British and world news, so having a short wave radio may be vital. In some countries, it is also possible to buy British or American newspapers or magazines, although they are usually very expensive. You could take out a subscription to weekly news summary magazines/papers such as the Guardian Weekly which covers British, French and US journalism and is sent by air mail. They will probably be eagerly read by other people as well. When things get unbearable, as well as letters and news from 'home', indulging in your favourite tapes, photos, soap, perfume, tea, coffee or sweets can help you feel better - so don't forget when packing to include a few little luxuries to spoil yourself sometimes.

LEAVING THE FIELD

As the time to leave approaches, you are likely to experience the same mixture of emotions that you had on arrival. there will be the excitement of seeing family and friends, sadness at leaving new friends, worries about your work (should you have done more?) and fears about getting used to life back at university.

In terms of practical matters, you are likely to have amassed a large amount of data, clothing, books etc. during your stay. Some of these will be vital and need to be transported home. Decide what you will need immediately on your return and make arrangements to ship the rest home. Do not let anything that is irreplaceable out of your sight! If possible have copies made of important data and carry them separately from the originals or post them home. You will also have things that you will not need again or can be easily replaced. This applies especially to clothes, but other such items include towels, stationery and toiletries. Friends and informants might welcome these and if you have any books to leave behind, a local library might be grateful for them.

The emotional aspect of leaving the field can be very difficult to deal with, especially if you do not know if, or when you will be returning. Unreliable or expensive postal services, illiteracy or an unwillingness to write letters can make promises of correspondence seem rather hollow. It is also worth remembering that although you may have made many friends during your stay, for most of them, your arrival was not a key event in their lives, whereas for you, the fieldwork experience may have been one of the most important things you have done. There may be, therefore, a difference in the expectations between you and local friends.

The central importance of time in the field does, for many people, lead to a 'reverse culture shock' once they return home. There may be changes in language and climate, and there will invariably be cultural differences. Feeling that nobody else understands what you are going through can make things more difficult, so if there are people in your department who have recently returned from fieldwork in the 'Third World', you might want to talk to them about how they are coping/coped.

Returning from the 'Third World' to the 'West', one of the aspects which many researchers find hard to adjust to, is the affluence in which many of 'us' live. Although there is clearly inequality within 'Western' societies, most people take basic services for granted. Anger and irritation at people's everyday gripes, for example about the transport system, and the waste of resources, such as water and electricity are common reactions.

Interacting with friends and family again can be difficult. There is a danger of becoming a 'fieldwork bore' as you recount tales of life in the field. Although it is incredibly important to you and people will want to hear about your experiences, be aware of alienating people - they may be bored, feel jealous or even worried that your enthusiasm for 'there' means that you are dissatisfied with your life and friends 'here'. There is also the frustration of not being able to really communicate your experiences and the disheartening realisation that many people do not actually want to know what your experiences were really like.

CONCLUSIONS

In this chapter we have tried to give prospective fieldworkers an idea of non-work-related issues you may face during your time 'in the field'. Of course, you may be one of the very few people who experiences no difficulties in adapting to life in a different country and culture, but for the rest of us, culture shock, homesickness and hassles with money are normal. Hopefully this chapter will have given you some ideas about how to avoid problems, or has convinced you that you are not the only one who sometimes feels inadequate and out-of-your-depth. Fieldwork is usually fun, but being forewarned certainly helps when the not-so-fun times arrive.

REFERENCES
Kulick, Don & Margaret Wilson (eds) 1995 Taboo: Sex, Identity and Erotic Subjectivity in Anthropological Fieldwork London: Routledge.

Martin, Biddy & Chandra Talpade Mohanty 1986 'Feminist politics - what's home got to do with it?' in Teresa de Lauretis (ed) Feminist Studies/Critical Studies Basingstoke: Macmillan, 189-212.

Massey, Doreen 1992 'A place called home?' New Formations 17, 3-15.

Oberg, Kalervo 1954 Culture Shock Indianapolis: Bobbs-Merrill.

Robertson, George *et al.* (eds.) (1994) Travellers' Tales: Narratives of Home and Displacement London: Routledge.

Wade, Peter 1993 'Sexuality and masculinity in fieldwork among Colombian blacks', in Diane Bell, Pat Caplan & Wazir Jahan Karim (eds) Gendered Fields: Women, Men and Ethnography London: Routledge, 199-214.

Woodlief, Mari L. 1990 'Oaxaca-Shock' in Martha W. Rees & Arthur D. Murphy (eds) A Student's Guide to Field Work in Oaxaca, Mexico Waco, Texas: Baylor University.

13.

USEFUL REFERENCES: READING, ADDRESSES AND FUNDING

General References on Research and Fieldwork
(* Indicates highly recommended)

Allan, Graham & Skinner, Chris 1991 Handbook for Research Students in the Social Sciences London: Falmer.

Adams, Adrian 1979 'An open letter to a young researcher' African Affairs 78, 313, 451-79.

Adler, Patricia, A. & Adler, Peter 1987 Membership Roles in Field Research London: Sage.

Agar, Michael 1980 The Professional Stranger: An Informal Introduction to Ethnography New York: Academic Press.

Bell, Colin & Newby, Howard (eds) 1977 Doing Sociological Research London: Allen & Unwin.

Bentley, M.E. & Herman, E. 1992 'Manuals for ethnographic data collection: Experience and issues' Social Science & Medicine 35, 11, 1369-1378.

Bernard, Harvey Russell 1994 Research Methods in Anthropology Second Edition. London: Sage.

Bulmer, Martin (ed) 1984 Sociological Methods: An Introduction London: Macmillan.

Burgess, Robert (ed) 1982 (reprinted 1991) Field Research: A Sourcebook and Field Manual London: Allen & Unwin.

Burgess, Robert 1984 In the Field: An Introduction to Field Research London: Allen & Unwin.

* Casley, Dennis.J. & Lury, Denis A. 1987 (2nd ed) Data Collection in Developing Countries Oxford: Oxford University Press.

* Clifford, James & Marcus, George (eds) 1986 <u>Writing and Culture: The Poetics and Politics of Ethnography</u> Berkeley: University of California Press.

* Devereux, Stephen & Hoddinott, John (eds) 1992 <u>Fieldwork in Developing Countries</u> London: Harvester Wheatsheaf.

Ellen, Roy F. (ed) 1984 <u>Ethnographic Research: A Guide to General Conduct</u> London: Academic Press.

Ellen, Roy F. (ed) 1984 <u>Research Methods in Social Anthropology</u> London: Academic Press.

Foster, George et al. (eds) 1979 <u>Long-Term Field Research in Social Anthropology</u> London: Academic Press.

Frost, Peter, J. & Stablein, Ralph E. 1992 <u>Doing Exemplary Research</u> London: Sage.

Georges, Robert A. & Jones, Michael Owen 1980 <u>People Studying People: The Human Element in Fieldwork</u> Berkeley: University of California Press.

Gilbert, Nigel 1992 <u>Researching Social Life</u> Sage: London.

* Hammersley, Martyn & Atkinson, Paul 1995 <u>Ethnography: Principles in Practice</u> Second Edition. London: Routledge.

Hammersley, Martyn (ed) 1992 <u>Social Research: Philosophy, Politics and Practice</u> London: Sage.

Heritage, John 1984 <u>Garfinkel and Ethnomethodology</u> Cambridge: Polity.

Kleinman, Sheryl & Copp, Martha A. 1993 <u>Emotions and Fieldwork</u> London: Sage.

Livingstone, Eric 1987 <u>Making Sense of Ethnomethodology</u>. London: Routledge.
Peil, M. 1982 <u>Social Science Research Methods: An African Handbook</u> London: Hodder & Stoughton.

Mikkelson, Britha 1995 <u>Methods for Development Work and Research</u> London: Sage.

Rose, Dan 1990 <u>Living the Ethnographic Life</u> Sage: London.

Sapsford, Roger & Jupp, Victor 1996 <u>Data Collection and Analysis</u> London: Sage.

Spindler, George D. (ed) 1970 (reissued 1980 by Waveland Press) <u>Being an Anthropologist: Fieldwork in Eleven Cultures</u> New York: Holt, Rinehart & Winston.

Twumasi, P. A. 1986 <u>Social Research in Rural Communities: The Problems of Fieldwork in Ghana</u> Accra: Ghana Universities Press.

Wax, Rosalie H. 1971 <u>Doing Fieldwork: Warnings and Advice</u> Chicago: University of Chicago Press.

Wolcott, Harry F. 1995 <u>The Art of Fieldwork</u> London: Sage.

Research Design and Management

Bell, Judith 1987 <u>Doing Your Research Project: A Guide for First-Time researchers in Education and Social Science</u> Milton Keynes: Open University Press.

Hakim, Catherine 1987 'Research design: strategies and choices in the design of social research' in <u>Contemporary Social Research</u> 13, London: Allen & Unwin.

Hakim, Catherine 1987 <u>Research Design</u> London: Allen & Unwin.

Howard, Keith & Sharp, John A. 1983 <u>The Management of a Student Research Project</u> Aldershot: Gower.

Locke, Lawrence, Spirduso, Waneen Wyrick, Silverman, Stephen J. 1993 (3rd ed) <u>Proposals that Work: A Guide to Planning Dissertations and Grant Proposals</u> London: Sage.

Marshall, Catherine & Rossman, Gretchen B. 1989 <u>Designing Qualitative Research</u> London: Sage.

Miller, Delbert Charles 1991 <u>Handbook of Research Design and Social Measurement</u> London: Sage.

Richardson, Laurel 1990 <u>Writing Strategies: Reaching Diverse Audiences</u> London: Sage.
Rudestam, Kjell Erik & Newton, Rae R. 1992 <u>Surviving Your Dissertation: A Comprehensive Guide to Content and Process</u> London: Sage.

Spector, Paul E. 1981 <u>Research Designs</u> London: Sage.

Particular Research Methods
Surveys
Barnett, Vic 1991 <u>Sample Survey Principles and Methods</u> London: Edward Arnold.

Brown, J. et al. (eds) <u>Multipurpose Surveys in Developing Countries</u> Paris: OECD.

Bourque, Linda B. & Clark, Virginia A. 1992 <u>Processing Data: The Survey Example</u> London: Sage.

Bulmer, Martin & Warwick, Donald P. (eds) 1993 (1st pub 1983 by Wiley) <u>Social Research in Developing Countries: Surveys and Censuses in the Third World</u> London: UCL Press.

Converse, Jean M. & Presser, Stanley 1986 <u>Survey Questions: Handcrafting the Standardized Questionnaire</u> London: Sage.

de Vaus, D.A. 1991 (3rd ed) <u>Surveys in Social Research</u> London: UCL Press.

Fink, Arlene & Kosecoff, Jacqueline 1985 <u>How to Conduct Surveys: A Step-by-Step Guide</u> London: Sage.

Fowler, Floyd J. Jr & Mangione, Thomas W. 1990 <u>Standardized Survey Interviewing: Minimizing Interviewer-Related Error</u> London: Sage.

Fowler, Floyd J. Jr 1993 (2nd ed) <u>Survey Research Methods</u> London: Sage.

Graham, Helen 1983 'Do her answers fit his questions?' Women and the survey method' in Eva Gamarnikow, D.Morgan, J.Purvis & D.Taylorson (eds) The Public and the Private London: Heinemann.

Henry, Gary T. 1990 Practical Sampling London: Sage.

Hindess, Barry 1973 The Use of Official Statistics in Sociology London: Macmillan.

Kalton, Graham 1983 Introduction to Survey Sampling London: Sage.

Leach, E.R. 1958 'An anthropologist's reflections on a social survey' The Journal of Hist. & Soc. Studies 1, 9-20.

Lee, Eun Sul, Forthofer, Ronald N. & Lorimor, Ronald J. 1989 Analyzing Complex Survey Data London: Sage.

Moser, Claus & Kalton, Graham 1992 (2nd ed) Survey Methods in Social Investigation Aldershot: Dartmouth Publishing.

Oppenheim, A.N. 1966 Questionnaire Design and Attitude Measurement London: Heinemann.

Rosenfeld, Paul, Edwards, Jack E. & Thomas, Marie D. (eds) 1993 Improving Organizational Surveys: New Directions, Methods, and Applications London: Sage.

Schuman, Howard 1996 Questions and Answers in Attitude Surveys: Experiments on Question Form, Wording and Context London: Sage.

Stone, Linda & Campbell, Gabriel, J. 1984 'The use and misuse of surveys in international development: An experiment from Nepal' Human Organization 43, 1, 27-37.

Interviewing

Beed, Terence W. & Robert J. Stimson (eds) 1987 Survey Interviewing: Theory and Techniques London: George Allen & Unwin.

Bernard, Harvey Russell 1994 'Unstructured, semi-structured and structured interviewing' in Bernard, H. R. Research Methods in Anthropology Second Edition London: Sage, 203-224.

Brenner, Michael, Brown, Jennifer & Canter, David V. 1985 The Research Interview: Uses and Approaches London: Academic Press.

Fowler, Floyd J. Jr & Mangione, Thomas, W. 1990 Standardised Survey Interviewing: Minimizing Interview Related Error London: Sage.

Herod, Andrew 1993 'Gender issues in the use of interviewing as a research method' Professional Geographer 45, 3, 305-16.

Kvale, Steiner 1996 InterViews: An Introduction to Qualitative Research Interviewing London: Sage.

Mc Cracken, Grant 1988 The Long Interview London: Sage.

McCrossan, Liz 1991 (3rd ed) A Handbook for Interviewers: A Manual of Social Survey Practice and Procedures on Structured Interviewing London: H.M.S.O., Office of Population Censuses and Surveys.

Oakley, Ann 1981 'Interviewing women: A contradiction in terms' in Helen Roberts (ed) Doing Feminist Research London: Routledge & Kegan Paul.

Platt, J. 1981 'On interviewing one's peers' British Journal of Sociology 32, 1, 75-91.

Ribbens, J. 1989 'Interviewing - An 'unnatural situation'?' Women's Studies International Forum 12, 6, 579-92.

Rubin, Herbert & Bubin, Irene S 1995 Qualitative Interviewing: The Art of Hearing Data London: Sage.

Schoenberger, E. 1991 'The corporate interview as a research method in economic geography' The Professional Geographer 43, 180-189.

Spradley, James, P. 1979 The Ethnographic Interview New York: Holt, Rinehart & Winston.

Focus Groups

Goss, Jon D. et al 1996 'Introduction to focus groups', Area 28, 2, 113-149.

Krueger, Richard A. 1994 (2nd ed) Focus Groups: A Practical Guide for Applied Research London: Sage.

Morgan, David L. 1988 Focus Groups as Qualitative Research London: Sage.

Morgan, David 1993 Successful Focus Groups: Advancing the State of the Art London: Sage.

Stewart, David W. & Shamdasani, Prem N. 1990 Focus Groups: Theory and Practice London: Sage.

Fieldnotes
Atkinson, Paul 1992 Understanding Ethnographic Texts London: Sage.

Sanjek, Roger (ed) 1990 Fieldnotes: The Making of Anthropology Ithaca & London: Cornell University Press.

van Maanen (ed) 1995 Representation in Ethnography London: Sage.

Key Informants
Johnson, Jeffrey C. 1990 Selecting Ethnographic Informants London: Sage.

Tremblay, M.A. 1957 'The key informant technique: A non-ethnographic application' American Anthropologist 59, 4, 688-701.

Participant Observation
Fine, Gary Alan & Sandstrom, Kent L. 1988 Knowing Children: Participant Observation with Minors London: Sage.

Jackson, Peter 1983 'Principles and problems of participant observation' Geografiska Annaler B 65, 29-46.

Jorgensen, Danny L. 1989 Participant Observation: A Methodology for Human Studies London: Sage.

Salmen, Lawrence F. 1987 Listen to the People: Participant Observer Evaluation of Development Projects The World Bank, Oxford: Oxford University Press.

Spradley, James P. 1980 Participant Observation New York: Holt, Rinehart & Winston.

Rapid Rural Appraisal
Chambers, Robert 1990 'Rapid and participatory rural appraisal' Appropriate Technology 16, 4, 14-16.

Chambers, Robert 1991 (2nd ed) 'Short cut methods of gathering social information for rural development projects' in Michael M. Cernea (ed) Putting People First: Sociological Variables in Rural Development World Bank Publication, Oxford: Oxford University Press.

Croll, Elisabeth J. 1984 'Research methodologies appropriate to rapid appraisal: A Chinese experience' IDS Bulletin 15, 1, 51-56.

Hildebrand, Peter 1981 'Combining disciplines in rapid appraisal: The Sondeo approach' Agricultural Administration 8, 6, 423-32.

Longhurst, Richard (ed) 1981 'Rapid Rural Appraisal: Social Structure and Rural Economy' IDS Bulletin 12, 4.

Studying Rural Economies
Connell, John & Lipton, Michael 1980 Assessing Village Labour Situations in Developing Countries Oxford: Oxford University Press.

Deere, Carmen Diana & deJanvry, Alain 1979 'A conceptual framework for the empirical analysis of peasants' American Journal of Agricultural Economics 61, 4, 601-11.

Harriss, Barbara 1984 Analysing the Rural Economy: A Practical Guide Discussion paper 164, Norwich: School of Development Studies, University of East Anglia.

Institut Pan Africain de Development 1981 Comprendre Une Economie Rurale Paris: Harmattan.

Auto/biography
Alpern, Sara, Antler, Joyce, Perry, E.I. & Scobie, Ingrid Winther (eds) 1992 The Challenge of Feminist Biography: Writing the Lives of Modern American Women Urbana: University of Illinois Press.

Denzin, Norman, K. 1989 Interpretive Biography London: Sage.

Gluck, Sherna B. & Patai, Daphne 1991 Women's Words: The Feminist Practice of Oral History London: Routledge.

Josselson, Ruthellen & Liedlich, Amia (eds) 1993 The Narrative Study of Lives London: Sage.

Langness, Lewis L. & Frank, Gelya 1981 Lives: An Anthropological Approach to Biography California: Chandler & Sharp.

Miles, Miranda & Crush, Jonathan 1993 'Personal narratives as interactive texts: Collecting and interpreting migrant life histories' The Professional Geographer 45, 1, 84-94.

Molloy, Sylvia 1993 At Face Value. Autobiographical Writing in Spanish America Cambridge: Cambridge University Press.

Okley, Judith & Callaway, Helen (eds) 1992 Anthropology and Autobiography ASA Monograph 29, London: Routledge.

Personal Narratives Group (ed) 1989 Interpreting Women's Lives: Feminist Theory and Personal Narratives Bloomington: Indiana University Press.

Scanlon, Jennifer 1993 'Challenging the imbalances of power in feminist oral history: Developing a take-and-give methodology' Women's Studies International Forum 16, 6, 639-645.

Smith, Sidonie & Watson, Julia (eds) 1992 De/Colonizing the Subject: The Politics of Gender in Women's Autobiography Minneapolis: University of Minnesota Press.

Stanley, Liz 1992 The Auto/Biographical I: The Theory and Practice of Feminist Auto/Biography Manchester: Manchester University Press.

Stanley, Liz & Morgan, D. (eds) 1993 'Auto/biography in sociology' Sociology, The Journal of the British Sociological Association special issue, 27, 1.

Sternbach, N.S. 1991 'Re-membering the dead: Latin American women's testimonial discourse' Latin American Perspectives 18, 3, 91-102.

Stubbs, Jean 1984 'Some thoughts on the life story method in labour history and research on rural women' IDS Bulletin 15, 1, 34- 37.

Yúdice, G. 1991 *Testimonio* and postmodernism: Whom does testimonial writing represent?' <u>Latin American Perspectives</u> 18, 3, 15-31.

Qualitative Research
Agar, Michael H. 1986 <u>Speaking of Ethnography</u> London: Sage.

Alasuutari, Pertti 1995 <u>Researching Culture: Qualitative Method and Cultural Studies</u> London: Sage.

Berg, B.L. 1989 <u>Qualitative Research Methods for the Social Sciences</u> Massachusetts: Allyn & Bacon.

Bryman, Alan & Burgess, Robert (eds) 1993 <u>Analyzing Qualitative Data</u> London: Routledge.

Burgess, Robert G. (ed) 1990 <u>Reflections on Field Experience</u> London: JAI Press.

Coffey, Amanda & Atkinson, Paul 1996 <u>Making Sense of Qualitative Data: Complementary Strategies</u> London: Sage.

Denzin, Norman K. & Lincoln, Yvonne S. (eds) 1994 <u>Handbook of Qualitative Research</u> London: Sage.

Eyles, John & Smith, David 1988 <u>Qualitative Methods in Human Geography</u> Cambridge: Polity Press.

Fetterman, David 1989 <u>Ethnography Step by Step</u> London: Sage.

Gephart, Robert P. Jr 1988 <u>Ethnostatistics: Qualitative Foundations for Quantitative Research</u> London: Sage.

Kirk, Jerome & Miller, Marc L. 1986 <u>Reliability and Validity in Qualitative Research</u> London: Sage.

Mason, Jennifer 1996 <u>Qualitative Researching</u> London: Sage.

Miles, Matthew, B. & Huberman, A. Michael 1994 (2nd ed) <u>Qualitative Data Analysis: An Expanded Sourcebook</u> London: Sage.

Morse, Janice M. 1994 <u>Critical Issues in Qualitative Research Methods</u> London: Sage.

Patton, Michael 1980 <u>Qualitative Evaluation and Research Methods</u> London: Sage.

Pile, Steve 1991 'Practising interpretive geography' <u>Transactions of the Institute of British Geographers</u> 16, 4, 458-69.

Strauss, Anselm L. 1987 <u>Qualitative Analysis for Social Scientists</u> Cambridge: Cambridge University Press.

Walker, Robert 1985 <u>Applied Qualitative Research</u> Aldershot: Gower.

Film/Photography
Ball, Michael S. & Smith, Gregory W.H. 1992 <u>Analyzing Visual Data</u> London: Sage.

Byron, Margaret 1993 'Using audio-visual aids in geography research: questions of access and responsibility' <u>Area</u> 25, 4, 379-385.

Collier, John 1986 <u>Visual Anthropology: Photography as a Research Method</u> Albueruerque: University of New Mexico Press.

Crawford, Ian & Turton, David (eds) 1992 <u>Film as Ethnography</u> Manchester: University of Manchester Press.

Rollwagon, Jack 1993 <u>Anthropological Film and Video in the 1990s</u> Brockport, New York: Institute Press.

Language Analysis
Milroy, Lesley 1987 <u>Observing and Analysing Natural Language: A Critical Account of Sociolinguistic Method</u> Oxford: Basil Blackwell.

Moer, Michael 1988 <u>Talking Culture: Ethnography and Conversational Analysis</u> Philadelphia: University of Pennsylvania Press. (conversational analysis in Thailand)

Time Use
Gillespie, Vivian Havens 1979 'Rural women's time use' <u>Studies in Family Planning</u> 10, 11/12, 383-384.

McSweeney, B.G. 1979 'Collection and analysis of data on rural women's time use' <u>Studies in Family Planning</u> 10, 11/12, 379-383.

White, Benjamin 1984 'Measuring time allocation, decision-making and agrarian changes affecting rural women: Examples from research in Indonesia' IDS Bulletin 15, 1, 18-32.

Statistical Methods
Kanji, Gopal, K 1993 <u>100 Statistical Tests</u> London: Sage.

Rowntree, Derek 1981 <u>Statistics Without Tears: A Primer for Non-mathematicians</u> Harmondsworth: Penguin.

Vogt, Paul, W. 1993 <u>Dictionary of Statistics and Methodology: A Non-Technical Guide for the Social Sciences</u> London: Sage.

Wright, Daniel 1996 <u>Understanding Statistics: An Introduction for the Social Sciences</u> London: Sage.

Other handbooks for particular statistical tests are published by Sage Publications (London) in the Quantitative Applications in the Social Science Series and Sage International Handbooks of Quantitative Applications in the Social Sciences.

Case Studies
Hamel, Jacques with Dufour, Stephane & Fortin, Dominic 1993 <u>Case Study Methods</u> London: Sage.

Stake, Robert E 1995 <u>The Art of Case Study Research</u> London: Sage.

Yin, Robert, K. 1994 (2nd ed) <u>Case Study Research: Design and Methods</u> London: Sage.

Yin, Robert K. 1993 <u>Applications of Case Study Research</u> London: Sage.

Miscellaneous
Dale, Angela 1994 <u>Analysing Social and Political Change: A Handbook of Research Methods</u> London: Sage.

Hill, Michael R. 1993 <u>Archival Strategies and Techniques</u> London: Sage.

Kellehear, Allan 1993 <u>The Unobtrusive Researcher</u> London: Allen & Unwin.

Lee, Raymond M. & Renzetti, Claire M. 1993 Researching Sensitive Topics London: Sage.

Majchrzak, Ann 1984 Methods for Policy Research London: Sage.

Mitchell, Richard G. Jr 1993 Secrecy and Fieldwork London: Sage.

Schwartzman, Helen B. 1993 Ethnography in Organisations London: Sage.

Stewart, David W. & Shamdasani, Prem N. 1990 Focus Groups: Theory and Practice London: Sage.

Walford, Geoffrey (ed) 1994 Researching the Powerful London: UCL Press.

Yamaguchi, Kazuo 1991 Event History Research London: Sage.

Gender and Feminist Issues in Research
(* indicates highly recommended)

Altoki, Soraya & El-Solh, Camillia Fawzi (eds) 1988 Arab Women in the Field: Studying Your Own Society Syracuse: Syracuse University Press.

Anker, Richard 1983 'Female labour force participation in developing countries: a critique of current definitions and data collection methods' International Labour Review 709-723.

* Bell, Diane; Caplan, Pat & Karim, Wazir Jahan (eds) 1993 Gendered Fields: Women, Men and Ethnography London: Routledge.

Bovin, Mette 1966 'The significance of the sex of the fieldworker for insights into the male and female worlds' Ethnos 31 (supplement) 24-27.

Cesara, Manda 1982 Reflections of a Woman Anthropologist: No Hiding Place New York: Academic Press.

Cotterill, Pamela 1992 'Interviewing women: Issues of friendship, vulnerability and power' Women's Studies International Forum 15, 5-6, 593-606.

Edwards, Rosalind 1990 'Connecting method and epistemology: A white woman interviewing black women' Women's Studies International Forum 13, 5, 477-90.

Eichler, Magrit 1987 Nonsexist Research Methods: A Practical Guide London: Allen & Unwin.

* Golde, Peggy (ed) 1970 (2nd ed 1986) Women in the Field: Anthropological Experiences Chicago: Aldine (2nd ed Berkeley: University of California Press).

Gurney, J.N. (1985) 'Not one of the guys: The female researcher in a male-dominated setting' Qualitative Sociology 8, 42-62.

Hammersley, Martyn 1992 'On feminist methodology' Sociology 26, 187-206.

Hess, Beth & Marx Ferree, Myra 1987 Analyzing Gender: A Handbook of Social Science Research London: Sage.

Kulick, Don & Margaret Willson (ed) 1995 Taboo: Sex, Identity and Erotic Subjectivity in Anthropological Fieldwork London: Routledge.

Lazreg, M. 1988 'Feminism and difference: The perils of writing as a woman on women in Algeria' Feminist Studies 14, 1, 81-107.

May, Nicky and the Networkers n.d. No Shortcuts: A Starter resource Book for Women's Group Fieldworkers London: CHANGE.

Maynard, Mary & Purvis, Jane (eds) 1994 Researching Women's Lives from a Feminist Perspective Basingstoke: Taylor & Francis.

McCarl Nielson, Joyce (ed) 1990 Feminist Research Methods: Exemplary Readings in the Social Sciences Boulder: Westview Press.

McDowell, Linda 1988 'Coming in from the dark: Feminist research in geography' in Eyles, John (ed) Research in Human Geography Oxford: Basil Blackwell.

McDowell, Linda 1992 'Doing gender: Feminism, feminists and research methods in human geography' Transactions of the Institute of British Geographers 17, 4, 399-416.

* Mohanty, Chandra Talpade 1982 'Under Western Eyes: Feminist Scholarship and Colonial Discourses' Boundary 2 12, 333-358.

Nast, Heidi et al. 1994 Women in the Field: Critical Feminist Methodologies and Theoretical Perspectives Professional Geographer 46, 1, 54-96.

Ong, Aihwa 1988 'Colonialism and modernity: Feminist re-presentations of women in non-western societies' Inscriptions 3/4, 79-93.

Panini, M.N. (ed) 1991 From the Female Eye: Accounts of Women Fieldworkers Studying Their Own Communities Delhi: Hindustan Publishing.

Papanek, Hanna 1964 'The woman fieldworker in a purdah society' Human Organization 23, 2, 160-3.

Radcliffe, Sarah 1994 '(Representing) post-colonial women: Authority, difference and feminisms' Area 26, 25-32.

Roberts, Helen (ed) 1981 Doing Feminist Research. London: Routledge.
Stanley, Liz & Wise, Sue 1993 Breaking Out Again: Feminist Ontology and Epistemology London: Routledge.

Sollie, Donna L. & Leslie, Leigh A. 1994 Gender, Families and Close Relationships: Feminist Research Journeys London: Sage.

Stanley, Liz (ed) 1990 Feminist Praxis: Research Theory and Epistemology in Feminist Sociology London: Routledge.

Warren Carol A. B. 1988 Gender Issues in Field Research London: Sage.

White, Christine Pelzer & Kate Young (eds) 1984 Research on Rural Women: Feminist Methodological Questions IDS Bulletin special issue 15, 1.

Whitehead, Tony Larry & Conaway, Mary Ellen (eds) 1986 Self, Sex and Gender in Cross-Cultural Fieldwork Urbana: University of Illinois Press.

* Wolf, Diane L. (ed) 1996 Feminist Dilemmas in Fieldwork Oxford: Westview.

Issues of Ethics and Politics

Barnes, John 1977 The Ethics of Inquiry in the Social Sciences Oxford: Oxford University Press.

Barnes Trevor J. and Duncan, James S. (eds) 1992 Writing Worlds: Discourse, Text and Metaphor in the Representation of Language London: Routledge.

Chambers, Robert 1985 Rural Development: Putting the Last First Longman: London.

Crang Philip 1992 'The politics of polyphony: reconfigurations in geographical authority' Environment and Planning D: Society and Space 10, 5, 527-549.

Ellen, R.F. (ed) 1984 Ethnographic Research: A Guide to General Conduct London: Academic Press.

Hamnet M.P., Porter, D.J., Singh A. and Kumar, K. 1984 Ethics, Politics, and International Social Science Research: from Critique to Praxis Honolulu: University of Hawaii Press.

Katz, Cindi 1992 'All the world is staged: Intellectuals and the projects of ethnography' Environment and Planning D: Society and Space 10, 5, 495-510.

Keith, M. 1992 'Angry writing: (re)presenting the unethical world of the ethnographer' Environment and Planning D: Society and Space 10, 5, 551-568.

Kohn, Melvin L. (ed) 1989 Cross-National Research in Sociology New York: Sage.

Kimmel, Allan J. 1988 Ethics and Values in Applied Social Research London: Sage.

Madge, Clare 1993 'Boundary disputes: comments on Sidaway (1992)' Area 25, 3, 294-299.

Mitchell, Richard, G. Jr. 1993 Secrecy and Fieldwork London: Sage.

Morales-Gomez, D. 1992 'Issues of ethics in international development: Dilemmas in social science research' <u>Canadian Journal of Development Studies</u> 13, 2, 197-217.

Porter, Gina 1996 "'Third World' research by 'First World' geographers: An Africanist perspective" <u>Area</u> 27, 2, 139-141.

Punch, Maurice 1986 <u>The Politics and Ethics of Fieldwork: Muddy Boots and Grubby Hands</u> London: Sage.

Rynkiewich, Michael A. & Spradley, James P. 1981 (1st pub 1976 New York: Wiley) <u>Ethics and Anthropology: Dilemmas in Fieldwork</u> Malabar, Fla: Krieger.

Scrijvers, Joke 1989 'Dialetics of a dialogical ideal; studying down, studying sideways and studying up' <u>Kennis en Methode</u> 13, 344-361.

Sidaway, James 1992 'In other worlds: On the politics of research by 'First World' geographers in the 'Third World'' <u>Area</u> 24, 4, 403-408.

Sidaway, James 1993 'The decolonisation of development geography?' <u>Area</u> 25, 3, 299-300.

Sieber, Joan, E. 1992 <u>Planning Ethically Responsible Research</u> London: Sage.

Western, J. 1985 'Places, authorship, authority; retrospection on fieldwork' in L. Guelke (ed) <u>Geography as an Intellectual Pursuit</u> Waterloo, Ontario: University of Waterloo, Department of Geography, Discussion Paper.

Winchester, Hilary 1996 'Ethical issues in interviewing as a research method in human geography' <u>Australian Geographer</u> 2, 1, 117-131.

Statements of ethical principles are published by many professional academic groups e.g.
    American Anthropological Association
    1973 <u>Professional ethics: Statements and procedures of the</u> <u>American</u> <u>Anthropological Association</u> AAA: Washington DC.

Useful References

As far as we know there are no similar guides to professional standards for geographers. The Association of American Geographers has found difficulty in developing a code of ethics (Bob Kates Feb. 1994 'President's column', AAG Newsletter, 29, 2).

The nearest to a statement of ethics by geographers is in an article by James Sidaway 1992 'In other worlds: On the politics of research by 'First World' geographers in the 'Third World'' Area 24,4, 403-408.

Autobiographical and Fictional Fieldwork Accounts
Barley, Nigel 1983 Innocent Anthropologist Harmondsworth: Penguin.

Barley, Nigel 1986 A Plague of Caterpillars Harmondsworth: Penguin.
(Both humorous novels based on anthropologist author's experiences in Cameroon - doubtful taste)

Bowen, Eleanore Smith 1954 Return to Laughter London: Victor Gollanz.
(Novel by Laura Bohannon based on work among the Tiv in West Africa)

Cesara, Manda 1982 Reflections of a Woman Anthropologist: No Hiding Place London: Academic Press.
(Soul bearing in Africa)

Dumont, Jean-Paul 1978 The Headman and I: Ambiguity and Ambivalence in the Fieldworking Experience Austin & London: University of Texas Press.
(Set in Venezuela)

Hobson, Sarah 1981 (1st pub 1978 London: J.Murray) Family Web: A Story of India Chicago: Academy.
(A woman's view of living in a family in southern India)

Hobson, Sarah 1973 Through Iran in Disguise London: J.Murray
(Woman's travel account)

Jackson, Michael 1986 Barawa and the Ways Birds Fly in the Sky: An Ethnographic Novel Washington: Smithsonian Institution Press.
(Fictional account from Sierra Leone about Kuranko African people)

Levi-Strauss, Claude 1989 (1955) <u>Tristes Tropiques</u> London: Pan/Cape.
(Accounts of field trips to South America)

Malinowski, Bronislaw 1967/1989 <u>A Diary in the Strict Sense of the Term</u>
London: Routledge.
(Revelationary diary by famous anthropologist about work among
Trobriand Islanders of Papua New Guinea - shocking for its self
doubt and racism)

Mead, Margaret 1977 <u>Letters from the Field 1925-1975</u> New York:
Harper & Row.
(Famous anthropologist's letter's home with lots of photographs - of
its time, but fascinating)

Rabinow, Paul 1977 <u>Reflections on Fieldwork in Morocco</u> Berkeley:
Quantum Book.

Reading non-academic literature (fiction, poetry, biography etc) about/by authors from your research region is often an enjoyable way to absorb a lot of background knowledge and understanding.

Health

Dawood, Richard (ed)1989 (2nd ed) <u>Traveller's Health: How to Stay
Healthy Abroad</u> Oxford: Oxford University Press.

Hamilton, Gervase 1980 <u>A Health Handbook for Volunteers</u> London:
VSO.

Juel-Jensen, Bent (ed) 1989 <u>Expedition Medicine</u> London: Expedition
Advisory Centre.

Ross Institute 1992 (frequently updated) <u>Preservation of Personal Health
in Warm Climates</u> London: Ross Institute of Tropical Hygiene. (copies
available from Ross Institute, Keppel St., London, WC1E 7HT)

Werner, David <u>Where There is No Doctor</u> London: Macmillan. (copies
available from Teaching Aids at Low Cost, Institute of Child Health, 30
Guildford Street, London, WC1N 1EH.)

First Aid Manuals are published by the Red Cross and the St. John's
Ambulance Association.

NON-ACADEMIC BOOKS
Travel Guides - especially the Rough Guides and Lonely Planet Guides are very useful and can be borrowed from public libraries. You might want to photocopy the most useful pages to take with you because they are generally bulky, heavy and expensive.

MAPS
It can be a good idea to make photocopies for maps you will use heavily in the field.

Buying Maps:
Blackwells Map & Travel Shop, 53, Broad Street, Oxford OX1 3BQ. Tel: 01865-792792; Fax: 01865-794143.

Stanfords Map Shop, 12-14 Long Acre, Covent Garden, London, WC2E 9LP. Tel: 0171 836 1321

Reference:
Map Library at Royal Geographical Society (1 Kensington Gore, London) aims to provide maps at 1:250,000 or better worldwide and is freely open to the public. Tel: 0171 591 3050

USEFUL ADDRESSES - ADVICE AND SERVICES

The Expedition Advisory Centre, is particularly useful in providing advice on planning an expedition. Workshops are run throughout the year:-

Expedition Advisory Centre,
RGS,
1 Kensington Gore,
London,
SW7 2AR.   Tel: 0171 591 3030   Fax: 0171 591 3031

Endsleigh Insurance supplies reasonably priced insurance to students abroad:

Endsleigh Insurance Services Ltd.,
Endsleigh House,
Cheltenham Spa,
Gloucs.,
GL50 3NR. Tel: 01242 258258

The Foreign and Commonwealth Office can provide information about the considered safety of different countries for British travellers:

Foreign and Commonwealth Office,
King Charles Street,
LONDON,
SW1

Advice to Travellers Line: 0171-238-4503/4

Interhealth is a medical charity specialising in travel health. It provides a travel clinic, health screening, health information packs and medical check-ups on return. It is a good source of cheap first aid and medical supplies like antimalaria tablets, water filters, mosquito nets etc. by mail order. It also publishes <u>Good Health, Good Travel: A Guide for Backpackers, Travellers, Volunteers and Overseas Workers</u> This costs £5.40 + P & P.

Interhealth,
Partnership House
157 Waterloo Road
London SE1 8US.   Tel: 0171-902-9000   Fax: 0171-928-0927

Key Travel supplies cheap air travel tickets for students doing fieldwork at charity rates:

Key Travel,
94-96 Eversholt Street,
LONDON,
NW1 1BP.

Tel: 0990-134-326
Fax: 0171 387 1090/ 0161-237-3456

Malaria Healthline provides up-to-date advice.

Tel: 0891-600-350

The Medical Advisory Service for Travellers (MASTA) provides health advice especially for people travelling to tropical climates.

Medical Advisory Service for Travellers,
London School of Hygiene & Tropical Medicine,
Keppel Street,
LONDON,
WC1

24 hour Travellers Helpline: 0891-224-100

Returned Volunteer Action
Produces a publication <u>Volunteering Overseas: Personal Perceptions</u> which researchers may find useful.
Costs £5.00 from:

RVA
1, Amwell Street
London
EC1R 1UL

Tel: 0171-278-0804.

Servas
A worldwide network of individuals/ families willing to offer hospitality to travellers:-

Servas International NI
PO Box 1035
Edinburgh
EH3 9JQ

Tourism Concern
"Aims to promote greater understanding of the impact of tourism on host communities and environments." Many postgraduates manage to combine their fieldwork with some travelling - Tourism Concern can provide information on how to encourage sustainable tourism where you are going to.

Tourism Concern,
Southlands College,
Roehampton Institute,
Wimbledon Parkside,
London,
SW19 5NN.   Tel: 0181 944 0464 Fax: 0181 944 6583

The Visaservice takes passports and documentation to embassies on your behalf. Details and costs are available from:

The Visaservice,
2 Northdown Street,
Kings Cross,
London,
N1 9BG.
Tel: 0171 833 2709

SOURCES OF FUNDS

The sources of funds mentioned here do not pretend to be a complete listing. This is meant as a starting point. It is a very good idea to talk to other postgraduates and those who have recently done research to find out how they were funded.

Major Award Bodies

The first place to start with in looking for funds for fieldwork is your major grant holder (if any) e.g. ESRC, NERC etc. But be warned - they require students to submit fully priced and itemised fieldwork budgets several weeks (or months) in advance of the fieldwork trip, funds may not be disbursed until receipts are submitted and may take considerable time to be processed, and there are certain items which they will not usually be funded e.g. purchase of expensive equipment like computers or vehicles, cost of research assistants or gifts to informants. Check the award handbook and fieldwork expense claim forms for details and if in doubt phone and ask.

University Funds

Universities may have funds especially for graduate studies, equipment, travel, expeditions or conference attendance. Check with your university offices and the head of department. In collegiate universities funds may be available from colleges. Student unions, especially their welfare sections, may be able to tell you what funds are available from within, or outside, the university. Universities now administer Access Funds which replaced welfare benefits to students - if your fieldwork means you have extraordinary expenses in a particular academic year you may be eligible for Access Funds.

Other Sources

Check your careers office for handbooks and directories of grantmaking bodies - make sure you check guidelines for eligibility and closing dates carefully. Read noticeboards in your student union, department, or college where details of funds may be posted. Try your local reference library too.

SPECIFIC FUNDING SOURCES

Albert Reckitt Charitable Trust

Supports about eight expeditions a year. Must be supported by the university and/or The Royal Geographical Society. For more information contact: The Albert Reckitt Charitable Trust, Southwark Towers, 32, London Bridge Street, London SE1 9SY.

British Federation of Women Graduates,

Several awards are offered to women registered at British higher education institutions. List of awards, application forms and forms for referees may be obtained from: The Secretary, B.F.W.G., 4 Mandeville Courtyard, 142 Battersea Park Road, LONDON, SW11 4NB. Enclose a SAE.

British Geomorpholoughical Research Group (BGRG)

Provides financial support for postgraduates who are members of the BGRG. This support includes small grants for research expenses and grants for overseas conferences. For further details contact: Prof. Ian Foster (Hon. Sec.), Department of Geography, Coventry University, Coventry, CV1 5FB.

Compton Foundation Inc

Supports research on population, environment, peace and world order topics disbursing US$3 million a year. Send for booklet/forms from: 545 Middlefield Road, Suite 178, Menlo Park, Ca 94024, USA.

The Developing Areas Research Group of the RGS/IBG

DARG offers a research travel grant annually to assist and encourage postgraduate students preparing Ph.D.s in departments of geography at British institutions of higher education to undertake overseas research. Application details available from Secretary, Developing Areas Research Group c/o RGS/IBG, 1 Kensington Gore, London, SW7 2AR.

Dudley Stamp Memorial Fund
This fund was established in 1967 in memory of Sir Dudley Stamp for the encouragement of geographical study and research especially by young (aged under 30) geographers. A total of about £3500 is normally available for these awards.

Application forms are available from the Executive Secretary, The Royal Society, 6 Carlton House Terrace, London, SW1Y 5AG and should be received not later than 28 February. The results of applications are usually announced in May. Telephone enquiries: 0171 405 7686 (Dr Chris Board, London School of Economics)

Gilchrist Educational Trust
Provides funding for British citizens working overseas, particularly on topics which are of potential applied benefit to the host country.

Guidelines and application forms from: The Secretary, Gilchrist Educational Trust, Mary Trevalyn Hall, 10 York Terrace East, London NW1 4PT.

Institute for Intercultural Studies
This organisation is concerned with intercultural and international relations and makes grants up to US$2000 to doctoral scholars for fieldwork and research. Applications from non-US nationals are welcome.

Institute for Intercultural Studies, Inc, Suite 1 B, 165 East 72nd Street, New York, NY 10021, U.S.A. Tel: (212) 737 1011.

International Federation of University Women, (IFUW),
Gives annual research awards to women working in a range of disciplines. Details from: 37 Quai Wilson, CH-1201 Geneva, SWITZERLAND.

Leverhulme Study Abroad Fellowships
The Leverhulme trustees offer annually a limited number of studentships for a period of advanced study or research at a centre of learning in any part of the world except the U.K. and the U.S.A.. Studentships are calculated on a basis of an allowance per calendar year for maintenance, a return air passage, a baggage allowance, and internal travel. Studentships, which are tenable for one year or two years at the discretion of the committee, may not normally be held in conjunction with other major awards.

Application forms are obtainable from The Secretary, Research Awards Advisory Committee, The Leverhulme Trust, 15-19 New Fetter Lane, London, EC4A 1NR. Tel: 0171 822 6964.

Monica Cole Research Grant

£1,000 is awarded to a female physical geographer undertaking original field research overseas. There is no age qualification, and both undergraduates and postgraduates are welcome to apply. It is awarded every two years. It will next be awarded in 1998.

Application forms may be obtained from: The Grants Secretary, Royal Geographical Society (with The Institute of British Geographers), 1, Kensington Gore, London SW7 2AR. Tel: 0171-591-3000; Fax: 0171-591-3001; Email: grants@rgs.org

National Geographic Society

The Society offers prestigious Ph.D. awards with no stipulations of nationality, or field area. Awards are frequently of the order US $30,000. The application form is long and can be obtained from: Committee for Research & Exploration, National Geographic Society, 1145 17th St, NW, Washington DC 200036-4688, U.S.A.

Newby Trust

The Newby Trust Ltd, is a grant-giving charity, working nationally, whose principal aims are to promote medical welfare, training and education, and the relief of poverty. Under these general headings, the directors have a policy of selecting one category for special support each year. In 1997/98 it will be Youth Education.

Further information can be obtained from: Newby Trust Ltd, Hill Farm, Froxfield, Petersfield, Hampshire, GU32 1BQ.

Population Council

Offers fellowships in the social sciences: graduate awards and postdoctoral fellowships for fieldwork/study each year in areas of demography, geography, anthropology and sociology. Write to: Population Council, Manager, Fellowship Program, 1 Dag Hammarskjold Plaza, New York, NY 10017, USA.

Quaternary Research Association

Provides funding for postgraduate students. For further information contact: Dr. P. Coxon, Secretary, QRA, Department of Geography, Trinity College, Dublin 2, Ireland.

Research Institute for the Study of Man

Provides funding for field research on race or ethnic relations, gender issues, education in comparative perspective, and problems of ageing. Different themes are highlighted every year.

For further information contact Dr Lambros Comitas, Research Institute for the Study of Man, 162 East 78th Street, New York, New York 10021, USA.

Royal Geographical Society (with The Institute of British Geographers)

The RGS/IBG administers a number of research grants, some of which are included in this list of funding sources. For further information contact: The Grants Secretary, Royal Geographical Society (with The Institute of British Geographers), 1, Kensington Gore, London SW7 2AR. Tel: 0171-591-3000; Fax: 0171-591-3001; Email: grants@rgs.org

Tropical Agriculture Award Fund

Set up by the Tropical Agriculture Association to raise funds in order to assist newly-qualified young British graduates in agriculture, forestry and related fields to gain appropriate training and experience in the tropics.

Further information from: Tropical Agriculture Association, 41, Redstone Hill, Redhill, Surrey RH1 4BG.

The Twentieth International Geographical Congress Fund

Annual awards from the 20th International Geographical Congress Fund are made to assist research and education for the advancement of geography in the United Kingdom. A total of about £5000 a year is normally available for these awards. Applications for grants from the 20th IGC and DSM Funds are normally considered by the same assessing committee. The 20th IGC Fund does not usually support postgraduate work for a Ph.D. thesis.

Application forms are available from the Executive Secretary (ref JECL), The Royal Society, 6 Carlton House Terrace, London, SW1Y 5AG, and should be received by not later than 28 February. The results of applications are usually announced by May. Telephone enquiries: 0171 451 2541.

Violet Cressey-Marcks Fisher Travel Scholarship

£500 is awarded once every three years to the best undergraduate or postgraduate research project which involves a period of overseas field research of more than six months. It will next be awarded in 1998.

Application forms may be obtained from: The Grants Secretary, Royal Geographical Society (with The Institute of British Geographers), 1, Kensington Gore, London SW7 2AR. Tel: 0171-591-3000; Fax: 0171-591-3001; Email: grants@rgs.org

Wingate Scholarships

Applicants must show that they are not eligible for Research Council, British Academy or major agency funding wither on grounds of nationality, age or residence, or because they will be working part-time, short-term or outside the UK academic framework, or because of the markedly original or cross-disciplinary nature of the project. Applicants must be (i) citizens of the United Kingdom or other Commonwealth country, Ireland or Israel, (ii) living in the British Isles during the applications period, (iii) 24 or over on 1 September of the year of application.

For further information contact: Wingate Scholarships, the Harold Wingate Foundation, 38, Curzon Street, London W1Y 8EY.

Winston Churchill Memorial Trust

Categories under which you can apply change every year. Categories for the following year are decided in July.

For information contact: Winston Churchill Memorial Trust, 15, Queen's Gate Terrace, London SW7 5PR.

Woodrow Wilson Foundation

Gives research grants to Ph.D. candidates researching 'women' and Newcombe Fellowships for studies of ethical/religious values. For further information contact: Woodrow Wilson National Fellowship Foundation, Box 642, Princeton, NJ 08540, U.S.A.

SOURCES OF INFORMATION ON FUNDING

Association of Commonwealth Universities <u>Scholarships Guide for Commonwealth Postgraduate Students</u> London: Association of Commonwealth Universities.

Association of Commonwealth Universities <u>Awards for Postgraduate Study at Commonwealth Universities</u> London: Association of Commonwealth Universities.

<u>The Awards Almanac: An International Guide to Career, Research and Education Funds</u> London: St. James Press.

British Council (annually) <u>Scholarships Abroad: Scholarships offered to British Students by Overseas Governments and Universities</u> London: British Council.

Cassidy, Daniel J. 1990 (2nd ed) <u>The Graduate Scholarship Book: The Complete Guide to Scholarships, Fellowships, Grants and Loans for graduate and Professional Study</u> N.J.: Prentice Hall.

<u>The Grants Register</u> London: Macmillan.

Ingleton, Elizabeth & Phillips, Patrick 1987 <u>Coping with Postgraduate Funding</u> London: Newpoint.

Silverman, Sydel 1991 'Writing grant proposals for anthropological research' <u>Current Anthropology</u> 32, 4.

DARG MONOGRAPHS

ORDER FORM: DARG MONOGRAPHS

	Price*	Number Ordered
No 9: E Robson and K Willis (eds), 1997 <u>Postgraduate Fieldwork in Developing Areas: A Rough Guide</u> Second Edition, pp 175	£5.50	....
No 7: R B Potter and T Unwin (eds), 1992 <u>Teaching the Geography of Developing Areas</u>, pp 143	£5.00	....
No 6: D Lockhart and D Drakakis-Smith (eds), 1990 <u>Environmental and Economic Issues In Small Island Development</u>, pp 134	£4.00	....
No 4: C Dixon (ed) 1987, <u>Rural-Urban Interaction in the Third World</u>, pp 177	£3.00	....
No 3: D Drakakis-Smith and S W Williams (eds), 1983, <u>Internal Colonialism: Essays Around a Theme</u>, pp 203	£3.00	....
No 2: M B Gleave (ed), 1981, <u>Societies in Change: Studies in Capitalist Penetration</u>, pp 163	£3.00	....
No 1: E S Simpson (ed), 1980, <u>The Rural Agricultural Sector</u>, pp130	£3.00	....

*   For overseas orders please add £2 to the price of each volume to cover posting and packing and make the payment in <u>Sterling</u> please.

I enclose a cheque (payable to Developing Areas Research Group) for

£.....................

Name:...

Address:..
....
....
....

Please send the completed order form to Reg Cline-Cole, DARG Publication Officer, Centre of West African Studies, University of Birmingham, Edgbaston, Birmingham, B15 2TT, UK.